OUTREACH and MISSION for VITAL Congregations

OUTREACH
and MISSION
for VITAL
Congregations

Dale Rosenberger

Anthony B. Robinson, Series Ed.

THE
PILGRIM
PRESS

Cleveland

Dedication

To my aunt and uncle,
the Reverend Andrew and Marie Rojas,
laborers in the vineyard of Christian outreach
to Latin America over five decades.

The Pilgrim Press, 700 Prospect Avenue, East, Cleveland, Ohio 44115-1100
thepilgrimpress.com
©2007 Dale Rosenberger

All rights reserved. Published 2007

Biblical quotations are from the *New Revised Standard Version of the Bible*,
©1989 by the Division of Christian Education of the National Council of
Churches of Christ in the U.S.A., and are used by permission.

Printed in the United States of America on acid-free paper that contains
post-consumer fiber.

Library of Congress Cataloging-in-Publication Data

Rosenberger, Dale, 1954–
  Outreach and mission for vital congregations / Dale Rosenberger.
    p. cm.
  ISBN-13: 978-0-8298-1728-7 (alk. paper)
  1. Missions. I. Title.
  BV2061.3.R67 2007
  266'.022--dc22
                                      2007012207

Contents

Editor's Foreword

As series editor, I am pleased to introduce this second volume in the new Pilgrim Press series on Congregational Vitality which focuses resources and attention on building and sustaining vital congregations as central to all that we are about.

The topic of this volume, outreach ministries of local congregations, is an especially important one for the many denominations. We are a people with a long tradition of service and advocacy who understand that our faith has implications for all of life. In particular, we have been called by Jesus "to love our neighbors as ourselves" and to seek and serve "the least of these" among us. Dale Rosenberger's contribution to this series will help congregations keep that tradition living and vital.

Dale comes to this topic not only as a pastor who has been particularly effective in engaging congregations in outreach, but also as a man whose family roots and history are rich in mission work and service in other cultures. Dale's own understanding of such work has been shaped and inspired by the witness of members of his family as well as his experience in congregations he has served.

As important as this family legacy of service and experience of congregational leadership in outreach are, Dale brings much more to the topic. He brings a keen theological mind and a Christ-centered heart. For those who have wondered how the outreach work of the church relates to our faith, this is the book! For those who have feared that at least sometimes the church's social witness seems like a cut flower, lacking living roots, this is the book! For those who long for their faith and service to be bound together in the experience of being part of the exciting movement of God's reign and purpose among us, this is the book!

All of this is to say that Dale Rosenberger has not only given us a book that offers stories and ideas for outreach ministries, he has done something even more important. He has written a book that funds such stories and ideas from a deep theological source and conviction. He will help congregations whose outreach efforts have diminished to sending money become congregations that share lives, thus becoming congregations that participate in God's great movement of healing and redemption. Dale will help you to rethink what you are already doing, and help you imagine doing what you had never thought possible.

As this series continues, church leaders can look forward to upcoming volumes. Our next volume will feature Talitha Arnold on worship; our fourth, Barbara Essex on the Bible and building biblical literacy in the congregation as a key to vitality. The fifth volume, by Martin Copenhaver, will draw our attention to discernment and decision-making in the church. We look forward to this continuing partnership in building vital congregations at the heart of the United Church of Christ and other denominations.

Anthony B. Robinson, Series Editor

One

As a Fire Exists by Burning

We could have resented it as an imposition and made excuses not to go. After all, the rest of the world was out that Saturday night, enjoying fine dining, seeing the latest movie, or taking in a play. But that night we headed 20 miles south to Norwalk, Connecticut. We carried a piping-hot homemade dinner for Pivot Ministries, a Christian residential ministry of men together finding their recovery from substance abuse. Because we had enjoyed a strong and personal relationship with Pivot for years, nights like this were fairly regular.

So it was not a banner Saturday night, as the world measures a good time. Then again, consistently cutting across the grain of the world's status quo and finding different kinds of enjoyments in unlikely places is at the heart of what it means to follow Christ.

It started slowly. The woman who ran the kitchen was bossy and the men of Pivot (who come and go with their graduations) seemed at first cool to one more church rotating in. More macaroni and cheese from polite suburbanites keeping their distance while assuaging their liberal guilt, they likely surmised. But as they sensed love cooked into the food, as former connections were renewed and scattered conversations sparked new ties, something fresh and powerful unfolded. God was building bridges across painful, yawning chasms of race, language, education, religion, culture, class, and neighborhood. And whenever the Gospel breaks out beyond the walls of the church and builds connections across such impassable breaches, where most refuse to venture, then the Holy Spirit is alive and moving. Then, look out world!

We could feel this energy swell as we headed into the backyard of Pivot's simple neighborhood residence. Their garage had been converted into a chapel. Worship always capped the evening after our bond with Pivot was renewed over dinner. And it was no mere token devotional either. Evening worship lasted well over an hour, including prayer, testimony, scripture, preaching, vocal solos — a vibrant, improvised, if somewhat homespun — celebration of Spirit. We white stiffs from the mainstream church would invariably end up caught up in this energy, going totally out of character, responding in kind.

We went to Norwalk that Saturday expecting perhaps to dip our toe in the water and edge into the shallows. But half-measures were rarely the order of the day as our lives intersected with Pivot Ministries. Instead we were swept out by sweeping currents, excited and surprised to find ourselves sailing in deep waters, charting a course through life with fellow pilgrims also seeking their way.

By evening's end, we drove home with a smiling, exhausted glow, having experienced a God-forged connection that we would remember long beyond any dinners, movies, or plays. We were energized, spiritually renewed, and the buzz in our cars was palpable. As after a promising date, we wondered how the romance of the evening could be preserved, prolonged, and shared back home.

Nothing about our evening was unusual or unique. Churches everywhere do things like this all the time, with little notice or fanfare. And these men from Pivot Ministries certainly did not count themselves as heroes, but as those who had hit bottom and were scratching their way back by the grace of God. At the same time, there is something truly extraordinary and astonishing about gatherings as simple as these every time they happen. Such events are not about able people helping disabled or less-abled people; not about the haves sharing with the have-nots; not about the fortunate helping the less fortunate; not about those who know how life is supposed to be lived helping out those struggling to get by. Such paternalistic, superficial benevolent-sounding talk often impedes God's reign as much as it postures at advancing it.

In truth, the Gospel is more mysteriously double-edged, more universally humbling, and more unsparing of every last person's desperate need for God than our best put-together faces and high-sounding talk lets on. And so rather than righteous people on one side helping poor unfortunates on the other, such outreach forays are rather about long overdue exchanges of spiritual gifts among differently gifted people. God has spread God's gifts around the world, forcing us to rely on one another and come together, to forgive each other's weaknesses and gratefully receive each other's unique contributions. God has spread God's gifts around the world so that we might reach across scandalous and agonizing social gaps and live out the unfulfilled realization that we really are all in it together.

Yes, many mainline church types can prepare delectable chicken dinners, hold down respectable jobs, balance our checkbooks, and get our children into outstanding colleges. But people like those at Pivot Ministries emerge from an edgy side of life that many mainliners have never seen, much less survived. The spiritual condition they must face in a state of permanent recovery has killed many. Do these soul-hollowing crises galvanize their faith into such simple, passionate dependence upon God? Probably. This much is certain: The light of God shines through the deep fissures running through the lives of the men at Pivot, and they willingly let that light shine. Of course, mainliners like me want to spackle and whitewash these same cracks in our lives for the sake of genteel appearances. The Pivot men have faced their mortality so directly they are disabused of such polite lies. Running out of time and chances, feeling their survival at stake, they can no longer afford the lies. Learning this is worth a lot more than even the best chicken casserole we serve.

That is why, for example, one of the most effective sessions of our year-long confirmation class featured the men of Pivot Ministries describing to our budding confirmands the difference God makes in their lives. Their talk was not some tepid lecture about being religious as one among many possible lifestyles. Instead their words bore urgency and passion about how God in Jesus Christ literally made all the difference for them between living and dying. The same is true of all of us, they insisted, even if your life is not at the moment threatened by substance abuse. Every decision you make, they proclaimed, is fraught with consequences for the reign of the true and living God or the worship of lesser idols. Where do you stand? How are you participating? Where are you headed?

So the men of Pivot Ministries instructed our young in areas where we were less skilled, comfortable, and articulate: our final utter dependence on God. Of course, to talk this talk you have to have walked the walk. The Pivot men had, and they held our confirmands' rapt attention. They had credibility and authority. They helped kids and parents in our too-full-of-itself leafy suburb get real in matters of faith about the actual state of relations between heaven and earth. They transported us to difficult but essential places we would usually evade and avoid. What wonderful gifts they gave us, in more ways than we ever fully realized.

Notice the nature of this particular exchange of gifts. We put out a nice spread for dinner on a Saturday evening, and helped them buy a new van. But they in turn would typically help us recover our charter of salvation in Jesus Christ, remembering who we essentially are — beloved children of God, no less dependent upon God than any of our neighbors. Mission and outreach, when they happen as they should, always engender conversion in all directions, especially among those of us who are sleepwalking through our faith pilgrimage. So, as I saw it, we got the better end of this exchange of gifts, despite that the "helpers" usually get all of the credit and the "helped" are often viewed as needy children.

And so if we want to talk about "need" as we talk about mission and outreach, let us begin by talking about our own need, especially if we live in an insulating cocoon of stability and security, whether urban, suburban, or rural. And let us talk about how being alongside those in crisis opens our eyes and clears our heads and reawakens our hearts. And let us talk about the church's need to remember who she is and regain her spiritual edge so far as embodying Christ's revolutionary message is concerned. And let us from our side confess these needs freely and up front — before we talk about the privations of the poor or the degradations of the broken — lest we become "do-gooders" roundly resented from all sides instead of servant leaders in whose image Christ shines, glorifying God.

"Wow," we thought as we drove home from Norwalk, "this really feels like the church! This is what the church is about! Here we know and see Jesus alive and at work in the world. Why don't we do more of this?" It may not be the world's idea of a good time on a Saturday night. But it is clearly God's idea of a good time.

Remembering Who We Really Are

Speaking of recovering our charter of salvation as Christ's followers, a parable helps us remember who we are, how the Lord has charged the church towards mission, and why God sanctions and blesses the life of the church:

> The story is told of a community of people who lived on a stretch of dangerous seacoast where shipwrecks often occurred. Eventually, some of the townspeople decided to put some time and effort and money into a rescue operation. A small life-saving station was built and the devoted members of the rescue team kept an ongoing watch over the sea, ready to use their little boat to search for survivors in case of a shipwreck. As the result of this volunteer operation, the town became famous because of the many lives that were saved.
>
> More and more people joined and became part of the team. Soon a new building was erected. It was much larger than the first little building, was beautifully furnished and decorated. And as more and more amenities were added for the members' pleasure and comfort, the new building was slowly transformed into a kind of clubhouse. As a result, some of the members began to lose interest in the rescue operation. But then a shipwreck occurred and many survivors were rescued and brought into the clubhouse for first aid. During the period of the operation that lasted for several days, the frenzied activity caused the attractive clubhouse to be considerably marred by such things as bloodstains on the lush carpeting. At the next meeting there was a split in the membership. Most members felt that the life-saving operation was a hindrance to the social life of the organization. Those who disagreed were told that they could build another little station further down the coast. And, as the years went by, history continued to repeat itself. Today, so the story goes, that seacoast has a number of exclusive clubhouses dotting the shore — but no one in the area seems to be concerned with rescue operations.[1]

In this context, the parable reminds us that the side of life exemplified by Pivot Ministries is the side that consistently drew Jesus' teachings, healings, blessings, compassion, and other attention. This side of life is especially dear to God's heart and God abundantly blesses it, if we are willing to open our ears to the Beatitudes and find blessing where they point us. In short, if we are to share our blessings with others and if we are to receive theirs, we must find ways to step into the breach, cross the social chasms that divide us, and bring together what the monied empires of this world want to keep apart. Finally, we who live on either of these two sides of life must find each other much more regularly and go far more deeply than the occasional Saturday night dinner and vespers.

Finding momentum outward from the church to enter such places of counterintuitive joy can be hard. But the outcome of joy awaiting us is real. Let me draw an analogy.

Generally, after a lengthy forced indolence because of sickness or injury, as I muster the energy to get out and take up exercise again, I am quickly exhausted the first few times out. In my still-weakened condition, I am actually draining myself of energy. In such moment, it is easy to question why I do this to myself. But, if I keep at it, things begin to turn. After a few sessions, I am reminded that I am capable of much more than I had let myself believe. Moreover, I find that exercise — rather than draining me — creates more energy than it expends. This experience, which runs counter to instincts of self-protection and self-preservation, is tough to explain and a hard sell to someone who has never done it.

This experience is also a parable for mission and outreach. Too often the church wants to stay within itself, thinking that, as things are, it barely has enough resources to get by, and that reaching out to others will necessarily involve further draining of the body of Christ. Some consider it distracting from more immediate, realistic, and pressing matters like fixing the roof and calling on the bereaved and shaping our children. After all, we all know that the world will never change, right? In a day when church buildings are falling apart, staff salaries are not competitive, and we lack time to do everything to maintain our ministries, it seems more practical to focus the expense of time and money within our walls.

But in the Christ-like self-giving that some churches stubbornly insist on, notwithstanding all the practical reasons why they shouldn't, these churches discover untapped storehouses of energy and liveliness. This is the power of the Holy Spirit loosed within a community and into the world. In obeying this impulse outward — where Christ has commissioned us — the church remembers the Master who sends us, remembers who she truly is, remembers what untold wonders she is capable of. None of this can happen unless the church is willing to step outside, get out of her four walls, and go beyond herself.

Taking our Pulse

In many ways, the best way for the local church to evaluate its mission and outreach is to take its own pulse: Do mission and outreach drain energy or create energy? So often the relationship of the rest of the church to this ministry has been, "Oh no, here they come again asking for our time and money. Quick, let's hide." Instead, this part of our ministry should evoke something like that feeling we had as elementary school children loosed for recess: "Oh, yes, this really feels like this church! Now we get to really live! Now we dig into the essence of what we are about!" In that moment, following Christ becomes adventure, faith finds its cutting edge pointing toward God's reign, and God's Word comes alive in ways otherwise impossible.

In 1982, adults serving the Westville, Illinois Trinity UCC youth group — less than ten young people — dragged them nearly forcibly off to hear Millard Fuller, founder of Habitat for Humanity, speak in Springfield, Illinois. .The young people went only because they were committed to the group, because we had talked it up for weeks, and because we had had fun so often before. On the ride across the state they were subdued, verging on morose, at the prospect of wasting a perfectly good Sunday afternoon in this way. When we arrived, the place was full and we sat in the balcony. They sat through the presentation quietly. But on the ride home, they were so animated in recounting what they had heard, the wonders of what God makes possible in the world, they kept interrupting each other, "And didn't you love it when he said…! Or how about when he told the story about…?" We smiled and noted the shift in tone and tenor from the drive outward.

The exercise and pulse-taking analogy works well not only for self-assessment but also for deeper understanding. Mission and outreach are indeed core practices of the Christian faith, a basic discipline in becoming disciples. And as we practice the discipline, despite our natural resistance, we find ourselves coming alive in ways otherwise impossible. We hear the voice of God calling us out of ourselves and into new places for good reason.

Mission and outreach are not options to be pursued as the church momentarily luxuriates in leftover time or money. Mission and outreach are core practices of discipleship. That is why it is so wrong to pit them against fixing the roof or calling on the bereaved or raising our children as people of genuine faith and strong character. In these various practices, we deepen our faith in different ways. Choosing some practices over against others misses the point. It's like a tennis player saying that the groundstrokes of forehand and backhand are real tennis while serving and volleying are somehow less essential. I would worry about that tennis player in the same way I worry about a disciple who professes not to have time, money, or interest in reaching out, especially to those unlike ourselves.

As we journey outward to places where Christ especially awaits us, the places beyond our comfort zones, we find ourselves not simply vindicated in our identity and calling, but also no less than energized, even galvanized. We take little leaps of faith that become giant steps within God's reign. Getting caught up in the greater drama of redemption rescues us from our isolated individualism and changes us forever. Once this gets in our blood and becomes woven into our spiritual DNA, we can no longer live without engaging the world on these reign-of-God terms where we enter into a new reality. So momentum is indeed a big deal in the realm of mission and outreach. And momentum needs to start in the church.

The paradox of mission and outreach is not unlike that of the burning bush through which God spoke to Moses, bidding him to go forward despite his doubts and fears, to leave his hesitation and inadequacies behind, to venture into the unknown of what God knows to be possible, and do something great caught up in a grand narrative of God at work in the world.[2] As we involve ourselves in freeing all of God's children for the fullness of living — and discover real freedom ourselves — we burn hot for the cause of holy things but are not consumed by it. And that this eternal flame will not extinguish, but only burns brighter in the darkness of adversity — despite inevitable discouragements along life's way — makes this flame all the more precious, wonderful, and mysterious.

Certain churches have a knack for taking on this characteristic burning-bush glow. And they become magnet churches attracting many, not because of how cleverly they work their market niche within our consumerist society, but because how the very light of God shines through them. Trinity United Church of Christ of Chicago, Illinois — at this writing, one of the UCC's largest and in some ways most dynamic churches — is a case in point. At 8,000-plus members, the warmth of their light has become a powerful draw for spiritual seekers and questers. Trinity UCC is also a bright light of hope for the mainline church in finding our way forward in a new day. So we look at them and wonder: How do you get to be a burning bush church?

A big part of the elevated expectations that Trinity UCC unashamedly places squarely before all of its members has to do with how they engage the world as people of faith. "There's a continuous reminder that we are supposed to be doing something," observes Barbara Allen, a long-time member who also served on staff. "God has put us here for some purpose. We try to help people find that purpose for their lives."[3]

From the get-go, new members are required to join up with one of the church's ministries, right along with being urged to tithe and to attend Bible studies. Yes, some of these ministries are the ministerial workings internal to Trinity UCC, like ushering or singing in the choir. Other ministries encompass legal counseling, HIV/AIDS ministry, single adult ministry, and prison ministries. There are no lines of demarcation in mission between what happens within the church and what happens outside of it. Mission is not what some of the people do some of the time. It is, rather, what all the Trinity people do all of the time.

Trinity's Pastor Jeremiah Wright has created a "Ten Point Vision for Trinity," points two, seven, and ten of which include a Spirit-filled church, a politically aware and active church, and a community-conscious and liberation-conscious church. So the example of Trinity seems to suggest that if a church takes people to the core of ministry in mission, something will ignite and burn but, rather than being consumed, will spread and grow. "If we don't get excited about the Gospel," Wright insists, "and if our people don't get excited about going to church, why would they want to invite anyone else to come?" Trinity has doubled in size seven times since 1972. That their mission is so clear and active is essential to that growth.

Holy Words Beg for Holy Experiences

The Christian practice of mission and outreach is at once grounding and soaring. Here we experience what Frederick Buechner eloquently described within our vocation as Christians, where our great need meets God's deep gladness. There is a rightness to this journey outside of ourselves in the body of Jesus Christ that we cannot know elsewhere. And if we are unwilling to go to the places where mission and outreach take us, large gaps will exist within our faith, like the isolated little child who has never experienced a birthday party.

17

Stanley Hauerwas makes the startling claim that we should consider not giving Bibles to the people in our churches until they have had experiences out of which the Bible might begin to make sense.[4] That way, the Bible might be less abused and distorted. That way, Scripture might be read with understanding, and the power of the Word might again become a force within the church. It is a startling claim for churches that place Bibles firmly in the hands of every third grader. But having been a pastor for going on three decades, I do understand why he said it. For example, take Mark 8: 35, right after Jesus' first invitation to take up his cross: "For those who want to save their life will lose it, and those who lose their life for my sake, and for the sake of the Gospel, will save it."

In a consumer-driven, I-could-never-possibly-have-enough society, where winning necessarily seems to make losers, words like these hardly have a chance. It is as though the Messiah spoke to them from another planet. What was he talking about? Oh, the words might conjure a faintly pleasing paradoxical ring of the mystery that sharing and compassion evoke, somewhere far beyond the worlds we live in. But entering this realm and grasping these possibilities with our daily decisions is about as remote from our lives as Oz's Glenda, the good witch of the North. They are simply not taken seriously because we lack the categories of experience to which they might give order and sense. So they merely evoke some remote, unspecifically benign, "spiritual, but not religious" feel-good glow.

On the other hand, if you have actually gotten outside of yourself long enough to have fed the hungry, identified with the destitute, nursed the infirmed, clothed the naked, or housed the homeless, then you do understand that in saving our lives we lose them, and in losing them we save them. Jesus' pregnant utterance names a precious part of your experience that does not get named elsewhere. He names a part of your spiritual yearning that cries out for some acknowledgement and insists upon further expression and development.

My younger brother Garth and his friend Steve spent a week in New Orleans, opening up homes that had been flooded and mudded six months previously by the devastating Hurricane Katrina. Going at their own expense and spending their vacation time at this disaster site, they pried their way into rows of homes to determine whether they could be salvaged or not. Along the way, they lived in basic tents, worked in sweltering conditions, and tore into damaged living spaces rank with unspeakable foulness, hardly able even to get a decent shower in the evenings. No travel company's glossy brochures promote this way of spending an all-too-rare week of vacation.

Nevertheless, tremendous esprit de corps developed among these reclamation teams, most of whom had never met one another before working together down on the bayou. Weeks back into their regular lives, Garth and members of this salvage team kept emailing each other. The message they heard consistently back and forth was that the time they had spent together, called by God and in service to neighbor, showed what it means truly to be alive. Getting back home to earn a living, while necessary, was something less, something more illusory, something less essential.

How goes the old saying? "Born a man, died a tailor." Many women and men sense God intended us to make a bigger difference for good in this world than being just another lifelong cog in mechanisms for profit. Many women and men at some level of existence recognize that the royal road to encountering and knowing God is through our neighbors. Our eternal destiny is mysteriously caught up in one another. And the more willing we are to travel outside our comfort zones to be with those unlike ourselves, the richer the rewards we experience along the way and the happier we make God. Discipleship is all about pleasing God and finding our own happiness indirectly as a byproduct of living out God's idea of what it means to be human, not our own.

If we truly wish to see the face of Jesus alive among us, he is readily glimpsed in the haunted faces of those reeling from apocalyptic devastation, hurricanes or others. That is why, when challenged about how to fulfill the law and the prophets, Jesus paired loving God completely alongside loving our neighbor as ourselves.

Want to stumble on and discover the meaning of your days on this earth? Lose yourself in places where life and death are most at stake, where the tectonic plates of the powers and principalities devour the innocent and grind the unsuspecting, where God's heart is especially on the line for people the rest of the world seems glad to forget. Want to move through your days only to regret expending as much energy in places as you did? Stay within yourself, keep to people mostly like yourself, and imagine that your own troubles are enough to keep you from venturing out to meet your neighbor in life circumstances so unlike your own. You can't learn the meaning of saving your life by losing it and correspondingly losing your life by saving it until you venture forth into such experiences.

Practice, Practice, Practice

Outreach is nothing less than a core constitutive Christian practice, as basic and essential as keeping the Sabbath, attending worship, reading the Bible, giving proportionately, forgiving enemies, praying to God, and telling the truth in daily living. As the example of Trinity suggests, when we invite new members into the life of the church, we should as automatically invite them to sign up for at least one mission initiative of the church as we invite them to remain regular in worship and their financial support of the church.

Thus, mission and outreach are not just giving away what excess we have leftover, not just benevolent and enlightened things to do, not idle gestures toward something as abstract as human rights, and not clever acts to fill out our resumes and make us look good. Christian mission and outreach are as essential to following Christ as anything else the church does. And if our faith will ever have much passion, it might likely emanate from this side of our walk with Christ as an affirmation of core conviction: "Here I stand; I can do no other!" At some level, everyone hungers that the abundant life which some enjoy be enjoyed by all. At some level, we all know that, because this is true, no real joy can exist for any of us until there is joy for all of us.

And if the church doesn't get out there and engage the fray — the fact that this world has enough abundance, but humankind badly messes up the distribution — then our lives may look Christian. If we cannot get over and outside of ourselves, we may bear the trappings of churchliness and the stained glass tint of righteousness. But in some final measure of things, our lives are only an empty shell. The apostle spoke truly when he reminded us that "faith without works is . . . dead."[5]

We, the church, have not always confessed this. Too often, the lifting of our calling to get involved and make a difference in the world has been perceived as an "extra" to be indulged because we are such good and generous people, because of social pressures like noblesse oblige, or because we must do our part as good citizens as the institution of conscience within our Christian nation. But the pulse and the heartbeat for what Elizabeth O'Connor calls "the journey outward" does not begin here.[6] It begins in the heart of Jesus Christ. And if we begin instead in these other places, our heart for those whom God stubbornly refuses to abandon will fail and we will come up short of the glory God intends.

As we will explore in the next chapter, our motives — why we do what we do — make all of the difference in the world. If we were to venture too far afield and lose touch with that heart of Jesus announced in the parable of the sheep and the goats,[7] we would not be adequately equipped for the journey. We would lose even before we begin in lifting up God's call to seek out and save, to be sought and to be saved. We would make the church singularly uninviting to uninitiated seekers. We would make the angels weep in heaven. We would make glorifying God in Jesus Christ as unappealing and useless and dank as doused embers.

Perhaps the Swiss theologian Emil Brunner said it best: "The church exists by mission as a fire exists by burning." Church and mission are indivisible before God. This is where our passion gets blood in its veins. Mission and outreach fuel the fire in the furnace that keeps us warm and searching of God's purposes in life's cold seasons. Mission and outreach keep alive and fan the flash of flame that is our burning passion for God's reign above every other power and empire. Once we lose these — the warmth of Christ's love and the heat of his passion for being true to one another — we have lost everything. Without mission and outreach the church ceases to be the church, and becomes a shell of itself.

A parable that Tony Campolo likes to use is helpful and instructive here.

There was a land where there was a great oil refinery. The refinery was gigantic and was known to employ all the modern techniques of chemical engineering. Its facilities were bright and shining, and those who worked there made sure that everything was kept in good condition and that everything ran well... One day, some visitors to the land asked to have a tour of the refinery. At first there was reluctance to show the visitors what they wanted to see. But when the visitors insisted, the rulers of the land directed that they be given an extensive tour of the refinery. ... After seeing the vast chambers for processing petroleum, the gleaming pipes that carried the petroleum products from place to place, and the extensive organizational system that had been set in place to keep the refinery going, the visitors asked to see the shipping department. "Shipping department? What shipping department?" asked the tour guide in response... "Why, the shipping department whence you ship out all the gasoline and oil that you process here," said the tourists... "We don't have any shipping department," answered the guide. "You see, all the energy products produced in this refinery are used to keep the refinery going."[8]

God calls us to be the source, not the drain, of spiritual energy, especially in the church of Jesus Christ, the community of faith fully and for all time empowered by the inexhaustible energy of Pentecost.

Walking and Chewing Gum at the Same Time

Let us be clear that, when we lift up mission and outreach, we are not talking about evangelism at the expense of service, or serving our neighbor at the expense of announcing the good news in evangelism. The activist and conversionist churches described in the next chapter set up false distinctions and choices like this, and we as the church end up harping at one another, frittering away energies and resources better expended on the front lines of need and opportunity. But the church that passionately confesses what lies in the heart of Jesus Christ for those especially beloved within God's intentions recognizes this as both divisive and false.

So this confessing church simultaneously maintains Jesus' Great Commission right alongside the Great Compassion, perceiving no conflict or contradiction between these two.[9] And this renewed church refuses to participate in the cultural tribalism that has so blunted the Christian church as a force for good within North America. For this enlarged church perceives the Holy Spirit moving seamlessly and ineluctably back and forth between these two great "Greats." And that annuls arguments and divisions, and reconciles our various ways of talking past one another, no less today than it did on that first day of Pentecost.

We have already observed that mission and outreach must necessarily always involve conversion — "ours" and "theirs," those who are sent and those who receive. Living out on this creative edge, where mission and outreach transport us, takes us out of our comfort zones and into a place where we come into a deeper dependence upon God and a more profound realization of what God has made possible in the death and resurrection of Jesus. This is at once personal to us in our individuality, and universal unto all in its social dimensions.

It is not as though we were not beloved of God before these conversions, nor that we were not necessarily "Christian," however defined. It is, rather, that we come to drink more deeply of the waters with which we were baptized, we come to find new satisfaction from those waters, and we come to trust their sufficiency to cleanse and purify and heal all of the earth, ourselves included.

My uncle and aunt, the Reverend Andrew and Marie Rojas, served as missionaries to Guatemala, Cuba, and, mostly, Mexico for five decades. They

22

taught in seminary, they started churches, they built up clinics, and they worked for the healing of God's people in Latin America. Uncle Andrew and Aunt Marie carried (sometimes smuggled) the Bible and its life-giving word into those remote places. Aunt Marie just as surely carried a piece of cardboard with her into the fields where the workers spent so much time, just in case someone went into labor and she would assume her role of midwife.

Whether delivering Bibles or delivering babies, whether saving intangible souls or saving infant bodies, it was the same good news of the Gospel by which the people they met came to glorify the name of God. It was the same power by which the covenant of salvation in Jesus Christ was reaffirmed and reasserted. It was the same conversion from trusting in the spirit of the world to trusting more deeply in the Spirit of God. Let no man or woman put asunder what God has brought together!

What Words Can Describe the Burning of Such a Fire?

So far in this volume we have used the words mission and outreach in tandem. It is no accident that these two words are so closely linked. We need both of them to describe the realities that we hope to treat within these pages. The word mission is important because it encompasses both the work of reaching out (e.g., "we have a mission to those suffering from HIV/AIDS") as well the larger guiding purposes of the church (e.g., "the mission of the church is to offer the alternatives of a counterculture to the tired, failed answers of the status quo.").

This dual meaning appropriately signals Emil Brunner's meaning: the church exists by mission as a fire exists by burning. For the work of mission in the first sense of the word cannot be separated from the overarching purposes for which God has created the church, infused it with life, and promised that it shall not fall — the second sense of the word. What God has in mind through creating the church is nothing less than serving God's purpose in redeeming this world from its fallenness and reconciling all who dwell thereupon. We glimpse the fulfillment of this destiny and the hope of this promise nowhere more than through acts which have traditionally been called "mission": the feeding of the hungry, the clothing of the naked, the visiting of the imprisoned, etc.

Sometimes people within our pews complain, "The church is not doing enough for mission." This reminder is helpful; we don't want to become like the fabled oil refinery of the parable earlier in this chapter, and we need prophets to remind us of that. But perhaps the tone of this complaint loses track of the fact that everything the church does — comforting the bereaved, preaching the word, teaching the faith, administering the sacraments — is consistent with the one and the same mission: redeeming the earth from its darkness and reconciling heaven and earth. Again, mission is not what a select few do some of the time on the periphery of the church's life as we edge out into the world. Mission is what all of the people of the church do all of the time in offering the realities that the church perceives as an alternative world where God dwells. And that brings us to the second word.

The word "outreach" is useful insofar as we need a word to describe the particular practice of getting outside ourselves as a people and finding those to whom God sends us for the exchange of gifts and meeting very different needs. In some ways, it would be better if we recast what used to be called the "The Mission Board" as "The Ministry Outreach Team," because that is more descriptive of the practices that this group of people hopes to cultivate with a given congregation. It would also be better if every board, committee, or ministry team had an outreach component, maintaining in our common life with our practice the dual nature connoted by that word "mission." But we are getting ahead of ourselves.

This chapter ends from the lofty, self-defining perspectives of the broad horizons where the next chapter begins. In subsequent chapters we will swoop back closer to the ground where congregations like yours and mine engage the fray and face the dizzying contingencies of how mission and outreach happen in the church of Jesus Christ.

Two

Paradigm Gut Check

The epic Teutonic tale *Parsifal* tells of the fortunes of a knight of the same name. After a watershed battle, still new to his vocation of knighthood, the hero in striking red armor seeks moments of repose. He briefly turns away from his quest and pauses to inquire after his mother's well-being. As he does, Parsifal happens to stumble upon the castle of the Holy Grail. But as he comes upon that singular goal of every knight, he is unaware of entering a sacred space. Some of the things we regret most in life happen when we are unaware that we walk upon hallowed ground.

Previously, as an apprentice to the rights and duties of knighthood even unto becoming a perfect knight, Parsifal had mastered self-control and moderation, basic disciplines of his noble calling. Less nobly, but as a matter of getting ahead, Parsifal had also been trained "*ir ensult niht vil gefragen*" — to avoid curiosity. So while at the castle of the Grail, he fails to ask King Anfortas about the special piece directly in front of him. That piece is truly special, the object of every knight's quest, the Grail itself. But Parsifal doesn't ask. The next morning he finds himself alone in a totally deserted castle, having missed out on the chance of a lifetime.

Failing to ask the right question just when it most needs to be asked, Parsifal loses this sudden, matchless opportunity. Decades of pointless wandering follow because he was unable to ask the right question at the right moment within the context of his greater quest.[1]

For the church of Jesus Christ, this legend is both instructive and daunting. We learn something important about ourselves and what is possible in our quest to carry forth the Gospel and somehow become instruments of God's reign. For we too suffer from a lack of curiosity about the nature of holy things we seek in the world. Because we have failed to ask the right questions at the right moments, because we have taken for granted where we are in the world and our place in the greater scheme of things, because we have shown puzzling incuriosity about things directly in front of us, we have missed incomparable opportunities. Worse still, we have wasted much time, not so much bravely seeking and questing, but sadly backtracking and wandering.

By contrast, the same Jesus who lifted that Grail was known for asking probing and piercing questions. He raised questions no one else was willing to ask, and did so at the least opportune moments. "Why were you searching for me?" "Did you not know that I must be in my Father's house?" "Whose image is on this coin?" "What does it profit someone to gain the world and lose his soul?" "Do you wish to be healed?" "Does this offend you?" "Do you also wish to go away?" "Who do men say that I am?" "Who do *you* say that I am?" "Could you not stay awake with me for a few hours?" "My God, my God, why have you forsaken me?" The result of Jesus' probing questions was to reveal his own motives and to expose the motives of everyone around him — both the godly and the ungodly — before God's motives on high.

Asking the right questions is the first place where Jesus found power and authority for ministry. Of course, it is all but impossible to find the right answers unless we ask the right questions. Perhaps that is why, even more than answering all of the endless questions of his followers, Jesus first and finally taught them to ask the right questions. Jesus' spiritual discipline of searching examination in all things allowed him to unite his will with the will of the Father until their wills became a seamless unity. And the Gospels repeatedly show us Jesus inviting his closest disciples to find their way after him by the burning light of this discerned and shared vision, challenging every pretender to God's throne.

On our good days, Christian people are still animated by the power of this purposeful union of the Father and the Son. We look to its wisdom and insight and power. We spy God's reign, if only in the distance, by the light of its shining city set upon a hill. We live off its clarity, its purity, and its singularity — how it bows to no power or principality — chasing away the demons of our lesser natures as we are so bold and crazy to attempt to be the people of God, to lift God's Word above every other word.

Motives, while wholly invisible and mostly inaccessible, matter greatly in coming to see the world from God's point of view. And seeing things from God's point of view is the first vital point in ministry. This is all the more remarkable given that we live in a world hell-bent upon expediency and immediate results, a world oblivious to what lies below the surface of things, what lies within. Let us make no mistake, in rendering God's wise judgments, God looks to the heart of our motives. And a lack of curiosity about our underlying motives and causes, our questions and greater lines of inquiry, as well as the models and paradigms out of which these intentions give rise, will not be rewarded in the realm of spirit.

Motives — our own as much as or more than those of others — must be exposed in light of God's motives and then adjusted and redirected. For to the extent that the motives of the Church remain unexamined in light of God's motives, our agenda will have little to do with the reign of God. If we pose merely human questions and accept merely human answers in place of divine questions and divine answers, we will be routinely co-opted by the world. Our quest will be sidetracked and we will spend years wandering in wilderness, wondering how we got there. We will scratch our heads and experience inward groans of sighs too deep for words over how we got so lost.

The tired old answers that result from asking the world's questions in that dying arrangement called Christendom, understanding our options only as they exist insofar within the context of the American empire, will not serve the purposes of God's reign in a world that has forever changed. Rather, if we cling to these tired questions we will find that little real ministry results, and that our ministry hardly evokes the high adventure or breathtaking quest of living within God's transcendent reign.

For the most part, the mainline church has been as incurious about our underlying motives and agendas before launching our crusades into the world as Parsifal was in the presence of the Grail. And, like Parsifal, we have paid dearly for it, having to double back the long way around just to return to where we began.

Purity of Motives Is the Key to Boldness

The issue of motive is also where many of the faithful grow suspicious and get cold feet as the church ventures out in witness to the risen Christ into the world. Many questions rise in our hearts, questions worth considering. Why is one particular frontier of our response important in this moment and not somewhere else? Whence does our action spring and where might it take us? What does it have to do with following Jesus? How does being Christian shape the means by which we respond? Does it originate in God's agenda for the world, or are other lesser agendas being cloaked here? In some hidden way, are we doing this for ourselves or for God? And whom are we trying to please? In the final analysis, being the sinners that we are, we must also ask, whose glory is finally at stake here? Is there anything of the Gospel in this? Or are we trying to show what good people and how we are part of the "right" crowd (usually people we perceive as like ourselves)?

When we fail to ask questions like these, so much of what we do by way of social witness ends up warmed-over detritus of culture wars. Failing to ask questions like these before engaging the fray, we have let powers and ideologies foreign to the Gospel frame the questions for us. The result is not pretty: liberals and conservatives, modernists and fundamentalists bundling ourselves up in the Gospel and wrapping themselves in the mantle of the Church while brandishing ideological interests that may have nothing to do with the cause of God's reign.

It is galling that many seem convinced that the truest expression of the Gospel could not be other than the liberal wing of the Democratic Party or the conservative wing of the Republican Party, in either case at prayer. Talk about a lack of transparency to oneself! That is how oblivious we have become to our own motives, and how invisible and worldly political agendas have infiltrated and used us. Over time, this plays out poorly. For as soon as those watching closely get a whiff that ideological partisanship is the mainspring of our witness — whether conservative or liberal — that witness is compromised and the Gospel is viewed with cynicism. And then the parameters of ministry encompassed by the church are no longer worth getting out of bed for on a Sunday morning. Should we be surprised that so many have made precisely this decision? Why not simply stay home instead and watch *Face the Nation* and get the same thing?

Usually people cannot articulate all this. They only sense it inchoately and back off, muttering under their breath and shaking their heads. They don't know what they're asking for; they do know what they don't like. "Not with my money, you don't," they say. "Not with my children are you going there." They turn away. "Not with my blessing will we send you." Nor are pastors welcomed as bringing something new and of God if we warm over yesterday's editorial pages of the *New York Times* or the *National Review*, if we wrap ideological political wolves in theological Lamb of God clothing.

This much is certain: God in heaven is not happy about how this distracts us from "the one thing needful." Nor are the people of God satisfied in the ways they seek to be in the church. A distracted and co-opted agenda must necessarily always have a short-horizon and time-limited run. And that is the good news of finding our impetus for exiting these fruitless wanderings, thanks be to God.

We say thanks be to God for not suffering our foolishness gladly, because counting on the world to pose the questions and narrow the range of answers shows pitifully little imagination. Also and more importantly, it shows pathetically little faith — certainly not the transformative and visionary faith of the Sermon on the Mount, certainly not the revolutionary faith that Jesus is still alive and at work in the world. Jesus had no need for the "parties" of his day, whether Pharisee, Sadducee, Essene, Roman, or Zealot, to effect his cause, and nor do we. We say thanks be to God because God would not be God — at least not the God in Jesus Christ — if God were to continue blessing and prospering the church for cozying up to disguised ideological agendas of cultural tribes where we feel comfortable instead of reaching for the all-embracing reign of God.

To put this more gently and place it within its historical context, for too long the only real question asked by Christians reaching out to the world has seemed to be, "What part of Christendom — the almost completely faded Christian empire — shall we prop up as its chaplains? Corporate or working class, white or ethnic, male or female, activist or isolationist, rich or poor, east or west, left or right, status quo or revolutionary?" We have been so obsessed with the endless variations of this question that we have been unable to let it drop in favor of new questions begging to be asked. Wandering lost through this Parsifalic time has been devastating to the integrity of the church's witness, never mind to our numbers in the pews on Sunday.

Caught Between a Rock and a Hard Place

Let us cast this epic struggle closer to home and more within a pastor's common experience. Having hatched a ministry plan to take the people of God out of their comfort zones and lead them into trenches on the front lines of God's reign, which pastor has not heard the reply, "We can't do that. It's too political." So often this comment functions as a conversation stopper, and worthy initiatives wither and die. And we never get beyond the dreamy-conversations stage of our bold initiatives to witness to Christ crucified and risen deep within the trenches of life.

Part of us wants to respond defensively, "No, it's not political; rather it's about the Gospel of Christ. The Gospel sends us to people and places like this." At the same time, another part wants to answer, "Yes, it is political, but only in the identical sense that Jesus was political. After all, one cannot live, breathe, or take a step forward without being political in one way or another." Which way do we turn? Clearly, new terms of engagement are in order here. And the good news is that at this moment the church lives on the cusp of these new terms.

Here is one example of living through this struggle. I remember leading Habitat for Humanity's Global Village Work Trips to Matagalpa and Esquipulas in Nicaragua during the late 1980s and the early 1990s. These were short-term mission trips, where groups of a dozen laypeople came together as teams to raise funds and build homes in the developing world. We then traveled abroad to build those homes with families and their neighbors, working closely under the aegis of Habitat.

My motives for going were manifold: My aunt and uncle had been missionaries in Latin America for more than forty years, and I wanted to follow up their tradition of witness in that part of the world. I speak Spanish and had extensively traveled in Spain, Mexico, and South America, but never Central America. Also, I was aware that Nicaragua was the poorest Spanish-speaking country in the western hemisphere. If Jesus meant it when he said "love your neighbor," I figured, these were our poorest hemispheric neighbors, so they bore a special blessing of God and an exchange of gifts was in order between us.

Finally, the common people of Nicaragua were deeply pinched in the fruitless geopolitical struggle of communism and capitalism. Because so much fear pervaded here, Habitat was having trouble recruiting Global Village Work Trips to Nicaragua, and so their Americus office asked if we would go. Amid the many distractions of the larger Cold War and the smaller Contra

War, little assistance was arriving though the need was so great. In sum, why not go where the need was the greatest, where I could speak the language, where many forms of Christian assistance were backing off because of the conflict, and where our efforts could do the most good? I was completely up front about these motives for all who had ears to hear.

Our trips enjoyed moderate success. As usual, aching backs, sore gastro-intestinal tracts, and homesickness created discouragement. But that was more than overcome by watching sturdy homes rise where people had been dwelling in sad dilapidated shacks. Even better, that warm glow in the eyes of Nicaraguans suddenly convicted by the truth that God had not forgotten them made everything worthwhile.

An admitted bonus was the silent satisfaction of sidestepping the geopolitics of the Sandinistas versus the Reagan Administration and doing godly work that would long outlast the demonizing political posturing on both sides. That felt like quietly and humbly serving as instruments of God's purpose in stark contrast to the strut and promise — and lack of delivery — of worldly powers.

One might think that little would be controversial about Christians going to build homes with the poorest of the poor. When we returned from Central America, however, I was unprepared for the polarizing ways in which the cold war between capitalism and communism and the hot war between Sandinistas and Contras distorted everything. Pastors, even those who knew me well, denigrated our trip and accused us of sucking up to the Sandinistas, of going because it was politically correct and *au courant* to align the church with the left-of-center revolutionary Sandinista party. One taunted me, "Was there a special line through Managua customs stamping the passports of church people [he meant sycophants, I think] like you?" In truth, we were rightfully skeptical about the Sandinistas, as we were certainly also wary of the Contras fighting them.

One woman in our group, Jan, had fallen hopelessly behind in her expanding printing business back home because of her participation in the trip. Having returned home and, still exhausted and queasy from the trip, working 14-hour days to catch up, she was blindsided by the response of a customer who asked why she had been unavailable for ten days. Beaming, she replied that she had been in Nicaragua building houses with the poor. The customer visibly recoiled, glaring: "Why, you must be a Communist!" She then telephoned me and asked how she should have responded, and words failed me as much as they had failed her.

The point of this story is how the theological politics of the Church and of the Gospel become so deeply entangled within the ideological politics of the world's empires. The point is how those around us have grown so tone deaf to the politics of Jesus, not having clearly and distinctly heard Jesus' radically transformative plea for so long, that they can hardly hear a voice such as Mary in her Magnificat (Luke 1: 46-55) without mistaking it for "Workers Unite" or "The Star Spangled Banner."

And you don't have to go to Nicaragua for a taste of this confusion. All any church leader need do is venture anything bold that would break down the many barriers of race, class, language, culture, religion, ethnicity, and the other walls that the world erects to maintain power and wealth as presently configured in the world. You will be soon consigned to some tidy niche of "us versus them" in the divisions of this world despite the category-defying, reconciling nature of the Gospel.

It is not just Jan and myself; all people of Christian faith need help here. Not that we expect the world to congratulate and reward us for doing Jesus' work. But we need better foundations, less confusion, and more shared interpretations of a common story amongst ourselves as we respond to those who would take us off task. For these challenges are actually opportunities for ministry, to point away from the pointless squabbles of the world and to point back to the reign of God.

Casting our Gaze beyond the Usual Suspects

What we need are new terms of engagement with the world for a new era when we still live in the old rubble of Christendom. It will not do to offer up some lame centrism between the poles of modernist progressivism and Biblical fundamentalism, take the best of this and some of that, a little this and some of that. No lasting peace can exist between camps which are predicated upon protecting a certain way of life, tribal groups bent upon protecting their own status quo, cultures clinging to their own rules rather than envisioning a world that bows to God's rule. Centrists mean well and can do good reconciling work. But here centrism means missing the inescapable point that we began with: One cannot get the right answers if one asks the wrong questions. A more radical realignment in the church's terms of engagement with the world is long overdue.

What we need are new terms of engagement with the world for a new era in the old rubble of Christendom. The old Christendom terms of engagement were nowhere better set forth than by H. Richard Niebuhr in his classic

Christ and Culture[2] Seminarians of my Baby Boomer generation were weaned on this book with its helpful typologies of Christ for culture, Christ transforming culture, Christ against culture, etc. I call them helpful because they articulated clearly and well the options that were available within the closed system of Christendom.

But now that Christendom has imploded, we must ask new questions to get new answers. Questions like: What are the politics of empires versus the politics of the Gospel? What are the politics of ideology versus the politics of Christian theology? What are the politics of Caesar/King/President/Prime Minister versus the reign that Jesus came to bring? These questions attest to the cyclical nature of history, for they resemble those that the church asked through its first 313 years of existence and that fell into disuse during the subsequent centuries of Christendom. Like the Jews re-settling post-World War II Palestine and pulling Hebrew from the scrap heap of history, can we relearn our nearly extinct theological language and allow this time-honored articulation on life and living to serve vibrant new purposes?

Back to the example of the early work trips to Nicaragua: I remember the day I announced this trip to my church staff. These religious professionals were decidedly unimpressed about the potential of our efforts to make a dent in the problem of such disgraceful worldwide housing for the poor. So I kept talking the logic of Habitat: how it wins over both Republicans and Democrats; how it refuses government help if that help means compromising their determination to present a fresh Bible to new homeowners; how the spiritual hope it engenders is even more important than the homes it builds; and how Habitat remains an avowedly Christian organization while also encompassing within its efforts those who care not one whit about God.

My fellow staff members were unimpressed. They looked back at me with world-weary, cynical, glazed looks. If you want to make a difference in poverty housing, they agreed, then you have to lobby Congress and state legislatures. There is no other way. That is where you must begin. There are no other choices. The scale of the problem is too great to be approached in any other way.

Similarly, beyond the confines of my own church, I remember as a member of the United Church of Christ's then United Church Board for World Ministries, raising the possibility of exploring a deeper partnership with Habitat for Humanity. After all, Habitat had begun in 1976 out of a partnership with the UCC's Indiana-Kentucky Conference. Why does the UCC now have so little to do with them? I repeated my request several times. It met with first indifference and then rejection. Dividing up diminishing administrative turf and fading mission funds, they didn't want to compete with Habitat's electric ability to raise funds. They knew that they couldn't compete in capturing the imagination of people of various political stripes.

Besides, they insisted, if you really want to do something about poverty housing, then you must present yourself to Congress, lobby hard, and make your plea before the American powers-that-be. If you want the barest chance to make a dent, you must lobby, win over an endowed government agency, and get the full weight of their funding. Any efforts apart from the nation-state (and its politics) are doomed to insignificance. Alas, Christendom politics are such a terribly difficult habit to break.

It is not my place to speak for the congresses and legislatures of our land. But I have seen pitifully little housing produced for the poor through the federal Department of Housing and Urban Development and its sister government instrumentalities in the three states I have lived in over the past 20 years. During that same time, Habitat for Humanity has built over a quarter of a million simple, decent homes for the poor worldwide, and the three churches I have served have contributed 53 of them. We have also had the joy of working on many more, everywhere from Danbury, Connecticut, to Valle de Santiago, Mexico.

What revolutions in society and the world would be wrought if every church built five homes with the poor? Or even one home per church? At least we wouldn't still be waiting around for a sufficiently enlightened Caesar or liberal-minded Senate to begin to do something that will probably never even happen. As with Parsifal, opportunities to glorify God in the unlikeliest places lay right before us, and we have missed them, expecting that life would be otherwise off in the mists of the future.

Road Maps to the Future Church

Speaking of the mists of the future, perhaps even the heavily-coded book of Revelation, wrested from the hands of televangelists who treat it as a made-for-TV movie about something called "the rapture," will take on new currency in the mainline church. After all, it is about the people of God attempting to live the politics of Jesus in the midst of and as besieged by a powerful worldly empire. Certainly we will never be able to understand the full range of options for how Christians had best deal with such powers unless we can learn to balance how chapter 13 of the Revelation to John describes Caesar ("I saw a beast rising out of the sea…") as against the words of chapter 13 of Paul's letter to the church at Rome ("Let every person be subject to the governing authorities; for there is no authority except from God, and those authorities that exist have been instituted by God

Perhaps the strongest book in reorienting ourselves toward new terms of engagement is John Howard Yoder's 1972 volume, *The Politics of Jesus*.[3] Yoder was decades ahead of his time and his work has greater currency now than ever. But because most of us likely will not read this demanding yet important work in its entirety, we might begin with a more immediate and accessible rendering. In *Resident Aliens*, Stanley Hauerwas and William Willimon summarize Yoder's typology for the church engaging the world.[4] They describe three different types of churches where we might locate ourselves, ask deeply curious foundational questions, and search out our motives before wasting our time and that of others. The first two types offered are familiar to us. The third church type is less so, but offers the most promise for our purposes.

The first is the *activist* church, whose motive is letting the church be the instrument for good in building a better society. Through more enlightened social structures and humanizing agencies, the activist church seeks to glorify God. The activist church rushes ahead to the transformation of the world without pausing first over troubling issues around the reformation of the church. Because the church has accommodated itself to the surrounding culture for so long, the activist church seldom takes seriously the radical nature of the Gospel, the call to discipleship, Christ's latent lordship over all things announced at Easter, and our empowerment at Pentecost.

Instead, it looks for the "cutting edge" of the Gospel in popular movements and counter-cultural causes to overlay and advance the Christian message. It calls upon its membership to see God at work for good behind social change so that Christians can decide to be on the right side of history and support justice as articulated within the enlightened politics of the nation-state — which today means the mind-numbing, fruitless squabbling between the left and the right.

The activist church values "raising consciousness" and believes that it perceives cultural crosscurrents from a loftier and broader perspective, so it seeks to read historical trends and selectively throw its weight behind progressive forces. Public morality is more strictly considered and gets more air time here than personal morality. The problem, Hauerwas and Willimon contend, is that the activist church lacks the theological grounding to stand above history and judge these vying powers for itself. Plenty of earnest and well-meaning religious activists were persuaded that Josef Stalin heroically posited a more just economic alternative. Even the great Reinhold Niebuhr came to view the Vietnam War as morally necessary within his highly contingent Christendom views of love and justice. More recently, UCC activists have spoken of Cuba in utopian terms despite its bloody and grim gulag system of oppression. Simply put, the politics of the activist church are too much spiritually retouched ideological liberalism.

The second type is the *conversionist* church. This church views the structures of society as hopelessly fallen, and is pessimistic about the church reclaiming and redeeming those structures from the taint of human sin. It looks askance at hitching a ride with secular crosscurrents because they bypass the biblical call to repentance before God and reconciliation with neighbor. Here private morality is more strictly considered and gets more air-time than public morality. The hope for collective justice and God's reign lies in the ever-spreading aggregation of personal conversions mounting up until Christianity takes on irresistible social momentum against all that would counter God's purposes.

So, from activist to conversionist churches, the sphere of concentration shifts from the public life outside to the individual life within. The front for action in the cause of Christ is not the social matrix but the individual soul. But because the conversionist church works only for inner change, it has no developed social ethic or vision of common life to offer the world. The conversionist church can seem indifferent or hostile to social movements, even those as widely acclaimed today as the empowerment of women and the treatment of every race as made in God's image. This church can also seem eager to bless the promiscuous use of military force and the motives of corporate America in putting balance sheets above the souls of human beings.

Indeed, righteous and upstanding members of conversionist churches in workplace, school, and home can quote Bible verse and call upon the name of Jesus while oblivious to matters that clearly outrage Jesus. And the political mandates of Jesus, such as those in the Sermon on the Mount, are displaced in favor of politics that degenerate into religiously glorified conservatism.

The third option is the *confessing* church. It is not some diplomatic mediation or halfway measure between the first two options. It is not a polite merging of hostile views to create a comfortable and congenial middle ground. Rather, the confessing church is a radical alternative to both activist and conversionist Christianity in the questions that it asks, in how it views our historical context, and in where it hopes to transport the church. In a word, the confessing church brings more of the independent moral and spiritual compass that the Church of Jesus Christ needs in this moment of fitful Parsifalian wandering, retracing of steps, and wondering which way to turn.

The confessing church is not about how to make Gospel more credible through tolerant secular institutions or through fleeting emotional dispositions of the human heart. It is less interested in working with the enlightened side of modern institutions to define ranges of our spiritual options. Its spiritual compass is more ambitious than trusting the power of momentary inward "Jesus spasms" to well up into a religious utopia. Rather, it forever and relentlessly presses the question: What would things look like and how would we act if we *lived* our confession that it is God, not the nation-state, who rules the world; that it is God, not legislatures, who defines what is possible; that it is God alone who sets the terms of what is at stake and gives us the vocabulary for sorting through our choices

The confessing church is doggedly determined to worship Jesus Christ in all things and let our theological political agenda issue forth from the place of glorifying and serving God. We can be sure that this theological political agenda promises, over time, to disappoint both the left and the right; it will also affirm certain particulars within both orbits. But in the confessing church, it is held that only the fire of unyielding worship of Jesus Christ as Alpha and Omega can hope to reveal the true parameters of ministry, whether in ordering our common life within the church's walls or how we venture forth beyond them in witness to the Gospel in the world.

What does such the confessing approach look like within the church's ministry? How does it approach the timely issues of our day in a different way? Here is a smallish example that nicely nuances the motives involved.

I know of a pastor who preached against the United States' invasion of and subsequent war with Iraq in 1993, the weekend before things broke loose, when nationalistic fervor was running high, somewhere near 90 percent approval, in support of the Commander-in-Chief's plan. Many other pastors counseled her not to preach an anti-war sermon at such a red-hot moment in history. She could lose her job or at least do serious damage to her pastorate. They, at least, did not plan to touch that tinderbox with a ten-foot pole.

She claimed that she would do so only in a certain way. She would not engage the issue of war along the lines of the left side of this and the right side of that, as most of the activist and conversionist churches did, directly or indirectly. That would only create a wedge within the church, importing the ideological divisions of the world into an already too divided church, much to the delight of the Evil One. Instead, her sermon sought to engage the matter of war on the church's terms.

She asked questions, hard questions at the heart of things from the view of the cross. When can the church admit that use of military force is the only option? Can we seriously follow Jesus and *ever* make such an affirmation? What is the history of the church itself — nearly uniformly pacifist for its first 300 years, and then afterwards the favorite religion of empire, during which time the terms of "just war" were set? What could we say about our own US government that would not so much pause over just war criteria in its haste to join the battle? Hadn't we considered just war criteria in the most recent war for Kuwait? What is the hubris of world empires when it comes to crushing their opponents and how did that factor into the decision to go to war? Clearly, the terms of the conversation were political, but she strove to stick to theological politics and eschew ideological politics, which was already filling and crowding out the public square.

She held sermon talkbacks after each of that Sunday's morning services so that her hearers would not feel trapped or ambushed by her message, but would enter these reflections as part of an ongoing conversation in a shared pilgrimage. She spent the afternoon telephoning the fifteen or so people who had either walked out of the worship services in protest or those who looked so stricken by her message that they were clearly in distress. One family, the biggest pledgers in the church, acidly retorted, "How could you as a Christian pastor not support our Christian President?" They would be gone in a matter of months. She could do nothing about that.

What was the upshot? Probably not much different than what many activist pastors faced in opposing this evil war, so destructive on so many fronts: *sturm und drang*, storm and stress. But remember, in the eyes of God our motives are more important than our results. In God's judgment, the means we employ in pursuing ministry are more important than achieving our ends. That sermon likely did shorten this pastor's pastorate in that congregation. But she did not mind, because dynamic pastors will always become enmeshed in conflict. And it is better to have conflict over things that matter than over trifles.

But then came the redeeming moment. The next day (the pastor's day off) at the exercise club, the head of the Board of Trustees approached her. It was an ominous moment. In his working life, this trustee had been a consultant to the businesses of both Secretary of State Donald Rumsfeld and Vice President Dick Cheney, and he professed affection and respect for both of them. "I probably disagree with almost all of the premises from which that sermon was written," this trustee gently began. "There is so much that neither you nor the church understands about the world at all. At the same time, I must say it is the job of the church to be against war almost all of the time. And you did a good job of that yesterday."

You could have knocked that pastor over with a feather. Here was a layperson with no theological education making a clear demarcation between the ideological politics of this world's empires and the theological politics of God's reign. If we take that lead, people will follow us and we will find permission to engage issues and controversies that we could otherwise never touch.

The Politics of Conversion

To be honest, one of the gifts of the confessing church is to engender conversion and renewal within and among us. Mainline churches don't talk enough about conversion, mostly because we fear that will come to resemble evangelicals more than we will become like Jesus Christ. But we can relax here because this conversion is of a decidedly different stripe.

This conversion is not about a pre-shaped and pre-approved emotional spasm that comes and goes. It is about altering our habits, patterns, and rhythms of life as God shapes us into a new people. Habits, patterns, and rhythms as basic as how we perceive life and what is possible, how we dare to tell the truth in a world of lies, how we will not forget about the poor and the broken, how we keep our promises because they are made before God, how we love even our enemies despite how we feel about them, how we would rather suffer than coerce or violate, how we would rather die than kill for what we believe in. Not only is this a distinct and singular set of politics apart from what the left and right have to say. These politics have the power to rally from all sides toward the cause of Christ in the world.

Conversion means trusting that what God is up to at any given moment in the world is more interesting and powerful than anything any nation-state is doing, even if these stirrings of the Holy Spirit are mostly invisible because such stories are seldom told outside of the church. When the church as community looks to God in ways like these, we discover new power — a power we cannot discover apart from the church. This power begins in Christ-like faith and vision. It ends in attempting things that the world says are not possible and finding ways where it appears there are none. In this regard, simply being the church is the most radical thing that we could do, and it is the best gift we could ever give to the world.

As the confessing church seeks to glorify Jesus in all things, it is the cross of Christ where the glory begins. The cross stands for truth come down from heaven apart from this world; truth around which all other claims of truth must be relegated; truth that begins and ends with God, exposes our idols, confronts the powers of death, and necessarily evokes the world's hostility in the process. The cross stands not for how God is willing to sit idly by and take what the world will give the church, becoming the errand boy for the world's little projects. It stands for how God takes on the world, on God's own terms, giving life palpable joy and people new foundations for their full stature in the loving sacrifices of truth-telling and "truth-living." The confessing church is faithful only insofar as it is the community of the cross.

Three

Make It Personal and
Watch It Become a Movement

As inconceivable as it seems, Dr. Martin Luther King, Jr. almost bailed out on his God-appointed calling to confront the racist powers and principalities in America's Deep South. When the official white powers of Montgomery, Alabama, moved to crush his floundering black boycott of city buses, Dr. King was caught up in the crackdown — jailed for driving 30 miles per hour in a zone of 25. Having championed a gentle moderation route of not-too-much-rocking-the-boat, asking for no more than what the inadequate segregation laws already allowed, King's reward was to stand behind bars in the company of vagrants and thieves.

The night of the next day after his release from jail was one of the longest nights of his short life. After a midnight murder threat — one of several dozen that day — King found himself walking the floor, alone and inconsolable. Normally he could brush aside the day's diet of intimidation and hatred, but this night it was getting to him. He felt himself waver. The specter of mounting violence brought him to the point of plotting a way out of the racial conflict without being branded a coward. Thoughts of all that his wife had sacrificed for his ministry and how his daughter could be taken at any minute left him trembling. It was in that moment when he realized that he couldn't call on Daddy and Mommy any longer; his father had actually opposed his decision to go to Montgomery. King was alone with God. He had waded into the shallows of a struggle, only to find himself within its deeps.

And so, in the timeless way of prophets before him, Dr. King took up the Power his parents had long commended to him, the Lord God, ever able to open up a new way when no way appeared. Head buried within hands, King bowed over the kitchen table, and prayed aloud.

> Lord, I'm down here trying to do what's right. I still think I'm right. I am here taking a stand for what I believe is right. But Lord, I must confess that I'm weak now, I'm faltering. I'm losing my courage. Now I am afraid. And I can't let the people see me like this because if they see me weak and losing my courage, they will begin to get weak. The people are looking to me for leadership, and if I stand before them without strength and courage, they too will falter. I am at the end of my power. I have nothing left. I've come to the point where I can't face it alone.[1]

As he prayed alone in that lonely kitchen, King heard a voice saying, "Martin Luther, stand up for righteousness. Stand up for justice. Stand up for truth. And lo, I will be with you. Even until the end of the world."[2] Then King heard the voice of Jesus telling him to fight on, promising never to abandon him, never to leave him alone.

King reached a place beyond fear and apprehension. "I experienced the presence of the Divine as I had never experienced Him before. Almost at once my fears began to go," said King of what later came to be called "the kitchen epiphany." "My uncertainty disappeared. I was ready to face anything."[3] These mysterious moments were as close as the genteel and intellectual Dr. King ever came to a conversion experience. In fact, it was exactly the type of conversion experience that all of us regularly need, which is not to say that we are not already Christian.

In this moment, Martin Luther King, Jr. went to a new place with God, a place beyond the barren metaphysics and scholarly equivocation of his Boston seminary lecture halls. He encountered something more vital than Yankee appeals to measured objectivity and gradualist prudence that had accompanied him southward after his northern graduate education. And finally in that moment he had a personal experience of a God actually worth worshipping as opposed to academia's more familiar "apperceptions of the numinous." Haunted and alone on that night, King experienced the God of his fathers, grandfathers, and great-grandfathers, writes Charles Marsh in his splendid book about God alive and at work in God-movements like this.[4]

King encountered the living and breathing reality of the personal God responsive to the deepest yearnings of the human heart, the God who both evokes and answers prayer, the God whose face we glimpse and passion we catch in the face of Jesus Christ. It is no exaggeration to say that, had King not gotten reacquainted with this God after his detour through the vapors of the historical-critical method and psychology of religion, the beloved and now-legendary difference he made for godly reconciliation in our land would never have happened.

Taking It Personally

When does bearing the Gospel into the world by word and deed become something personal for us? At what point do we turn to the true and living God of the cross, realizing that our fleeting, seemingly-prominent little gods amount to nothing, like King's gods who dissipated that night at his kitchen table? When do we get up and answer the indignities the world foists upon those broken and forgotten to the world, but beloved to God's heart — when are we no longer content to play defense, backpedaling so that no one will get hurt, but instead actually move to the offense, lifting up essential truths no one else will speak? If we fail to ask these questions aloud of each other in the church, King's life and example instruct us, then nothing great or substantial for the cause of God's reign will result from our days. And that is the biggest disappointment we could know within our lifetime.

Where would we risk what is most precious and cherished to us for the cause of God's reign? Where would we put ourselves on the line in a religion whose symbol is not a Barcalounger with a remote control on the arm, but a cross fraught with personal risk and possibility? At what point does the authority of God's crucified and resurrected Son touch us in a ways that overrides the plans we have invested in mutual funds, pension accounts, insurance policies, and inheritances?

The German Reformer Martin Luther, after whom Dr. King was named, asserted that we can tell what people truly believe by what we are willing to sacrifice their children for. Do we sacrifice our young that they might carry forward the legacy of Fortune 500 corporations or that all people of the world might know themselves as children of God for whom Christ lived and died? It's hard to imagine saying anything that would make the terms of what is at stake more personal than that. And if the impulse sending us outward to do God's work in alien places has not yet become deeply and incontrovertibly personal, then the Holy Spirit still has not fully empowered us to do what we need to do.

Where would our walk with Jesus Christ become something more than a lifestyle choice like joining the garden club? When would we let the influence of the church and its mission into the world override the plans we make around the soccer games for our children, the weekends at the lake in our friend's cabin, the hoping and scheming after the family inheritance, or the coveted Christmas break time-shares in Florida? How would we substantially rebut the perpetual fear Jesus articulated in quoting from Isaiah: "Because these people draw near with their mouths and honor me with their lips, while their hearts are far from me, and their worship of me is a human commandment learned by rote"?[5]

It is far easier than we imagine to spend an entire lifetime without seriously weighing and participating in the only dimension of life that is permanent: the realm of spirit, the land where Jesus takes us. It is far too easy merely to dabble or to skim across the surface of a life in God's Spirit. Yes, this happens even among those who hang out at the church. I see this disappointment all the time and, if it saddens me, I cannot imagine how sad it must be to live this way. The mission and outreach of the church hold more power and potential for correcting this spiritual deficit than can be found anywhere else in our daily routine.

Unlike Dr. King, the temptation of the mainline church is not so much to get lost in the high-flown, ethereal abstractions of the metaphysical. Rather, our temptation is to enter the low-flown, rat-maze proceduralism of the bureaucratic, never to reemerge as the people we were before we entered that grey space. Once we become above all institutional, we squeeze out so much adventure, personality, vitality, encounter, discovery, spontaneity — everything that personalizes our discipleship. And once we become entrenched in our institutionalism, so much of our time, energy, money, and other resources invariably get sunk into preserving the institutional status quo, as sketched by the parable of the life-saving station in Chapter One. Institutional maintenance is not benign or neutral. It actually prevents us from getting out into those essential places where Jesus lived and invited us to serve.

I have never met anyone in church who repeatedly lifts up *Robert's Rules of Order* in one hand as the key document for the church and yet who simultaneously, in the other hand, also waves the Bible in ways that capture the imagination and compel outward, holy, compassionate, generous acts of service. Rather, I have experienced much more often those who brandish by-laws as hijacking the mission upon which the Bible sends us, pulling us back, keeping us prudent, lifting up institutional security as a heroic contribution to protect the church from the loonies who actually believe that we should be saying and doing the very things that Jesus said and did.

A servant cannot serve two masters. This is true not just of God and mammon. It is also true for God and that brand of institutional security. As we observed earlier, protecting the status quo as a form of keeping ourselves secure is perhaps the greatest idol of them all. The mind-set where human comfort and control reign allows no room for God's reign. If we are hell-bent upon preserving the church as an institution with its constitution, by-laws, and officers, then we cannot expect to get caught up in the church as a personal, passionate, guerrillas-by-grace movement against powers and principalities with its prophet leaders.

Again, the good news here is that the church's vibrant and active mission and outreach is the most potently transformative elixir here, known to turn bespectacled accountants into bulldogs for debt relief in the developing world. More will be said on this and examples will be summoned on understanding the church as movement (as opposed to institution) later in this chapter. But first let us more fully diagnose and comprehend what it means to devolve into being a procedural church.

Putting Some Color Back into our Cheeks

My friend Martin Copenhaver likes to observe that his vision of hell is having everything that we have in the church — boards, committees, potlucks, annual meetings, auctions, commissions, teas — but without Jesus Christ. This is *corruptio optimi pessimi*, the corruption of the very best things leaving the very worst of things. Here the worst thing is remaining an institutional shell while living without the vision and drive and moral purpose that true life in Jesus Christ must compel.

Another friend, Anthony Robinson, wrote compellingly about such a church after the Twenty-first General Synod of the United Church of Christ. Bouncing his queries off those asked by political scientists, Robinson observed that the UCC is replete with rights, rules, and procedures, but to what end?[6] At the national level, he observed a church obsessed with coalitions, restructuring, agreements, instrumentalities, commissions, and constitutions. When changes occurred in these areas at the Synod, little or no debate resulted. Why? Clearly because the delegates sensed so little at stake.

Tony went on to note that whenever we talked about issues like race and racism, we did so "through the lens and in the language of contemporary, secular culture. That language, mostly psychotherapeutic, and not the language of the New Testament, set the terms of the discussion. There was no suggestion that the church struggling to be multi-cultural and multi-racial might find guidance, as well as challenge, from the Book of Acts or from Paul's letter to the Romans or the Galatians."[7]

Sadly, nature doesn't tolerate a vacuum. So catch phrases such as "inclusive" or "just peace" or "multi-cultural" or "multi-racial" replace any biblical or theological considerations. And once these shibboleths invade and conquer, they set themselves up as litmus tests to be enforced with a vigor that is no less than liberal fundamentalism, the left side of this mocking the right side of that.

What does all this mean to the local church? It is deeply ironic that in the free-church tradition where we stand, we have choked ourselves on polity and organization, the antithesis of freedom as the Holy Spirit reveals it. The very processes meant to liberate our deliberations and propel our initiatives forward have instead imprisoned us, as these procedures have become sacrosanct — holy cows lumbering through corridors and congregational meetings. Instead of shaping our outreach in ways that Jesus commanded,[8] not heavily burdened by carrying too much personal baggage, our impulse toward mission has become freighted by a ponderous way of doing things that makes energetic, excited, and eager newcomers to our churches wonder what went wrong. What is holding us back? they ask, having been invited into the wonder of a church that indwells Gospel mysteries and then finding themselves spending long minutes fussing over last month's minutes.

How has this come about? It is not difficult to see. Out of the old Christendom paradigms for mission and outreach, we have organized our work in outreach within the church as though the leaders on these board and committees were a mini-National Council of Churches or World Council of Churches. These groups then increasingly see themselves as panels whose job it is to relate to Christian-friendly benevolences, to establish policies internal to the church, to allocate money in their direction, and to set in to motion all of the waiting impulses in what used to be a Christian-friendly environment. Like the people in the life-saving station of Chapter One, they don't actually do mission and outreach anymore. They have a faint memory of when that used to happen. But with "the advances of modern times," all of that is behind us now. Instead, they mostly relate to others whose organization somehow touches the suffering and opportunity of the world on the church's behalf.

What we end up with in this arrangement — whether we speak of the mainline denominations or the local church — is agency talking to agency, institution relating to institution, representatives talking to other representatives, instrumentality stroking instrumentality. And every time it is with visions of a better world, a godlier world, even the very reign of God, but always with someone else putting her- or himself on the line. When does this become personal to us? When do we step out and put ourselves into the trenches where transformation happens? In the meantime, those who await an encouraging word or a saving touch from the body of Christ somehow remain invisible and get lost within a well-insulated bureaucracy. What we end up with is a procedural church.

What that Feels Like

I remember a sinking feeling before my sabbatical to Costa Rica in 1990. My family and I were traveling to San Jose for four months where I would study in a local seminary and rehabilitate my Spanish. Already carrying the bags for myself and for two pre-school children, I didn't really want to add any more to the accoutrements of our family caravan. But a seminary professor and member of our church, Dr. Sharon Ringe, insisted that I call the UCC's national offices in Cleveland and ask how I might be a helpful go-between to mission partners in Central America. Having served six years on the United Church Board for World Ministries and with the church's mission in my blood from my early upbringing, I agreed that it was the right thing to do.

So I called Cleveland. From praying my Calendar of Prayer, I knew that the UCC had a mission presence in San Jose, or at least a relationship with an ecumenical church group there of a kind that I didn't quite understand. No matter. I spoke to a high church officer. How can I be helpful? What can I do? Is there any material that I might transport? (Shipping things is difficult, expensive, and risky throughout Latin America.) It could be office supplies, medicine, perhaps something fragile like electronics to deliver to a related office. Surely I could at least bring greetings to someone. Let me know how I can make a difference, since I am already headed there.

I was surprised by the vigor with which I was assailed for my sugges-tion. Who did I think I was, imagining that I could represent the complex deliberations of a national church? What did I really know about global mis-sion? We can't have every Tom, Dick, and Harry running around down there in our name. I had thought that I was a disciple of Jesus Christ and that we were together in this thing called mission and outreach, pulling in the same direction. But I quickly learned this was wrong. And I wondered: if I, a pas-tor-veteran of our UCC's world mission board, got shot down like this, what kind of reception would await the average layperson seeking to connect with the church's extended mission? This is a small story, but enough to make me lament over the church's fall from personal to procedural.

As soon as we who profess mission distance ourselves from immediate acts of doing outreach ourselves and insulate ourselves with layers of admin-istration and agencies whom we trust to act in God's name on our behalf, we are set up for a fall — no, more precisely, we are doomed. And it is a long, hard fall from what Jesus intended when he sent out those seventy disciples two-by-two.

What would it look like for the church to move beyond the Christendom paradigm for doing mission toward something more personal and confes-sional? How can we reshape ourselves from what we have become back into what we once were? How can mission and outreach become more passionate and less institutional? Here are a few starting points, or at least conversation points, in our drive to deinstitutionalize mission and outreach, and to put some blood back into our cheeks:

• Replace the church's Mission Board or Committee, which usually administers the church's mission like an agency, with a ministry team such as might run a small worship service within your church. Maybe mission teams in the plural, one for local outreach perhaps, another for more global responses, another for dealing with denominational opportunities to make a difference, and so forth. Many nominating committee are already having problems filling classical Mission Board spots, and many who are asked to serve are skipping the meetings anyway — they wanted to do outreach but find themselves being simply administrators. Ministry teams can turn this around. Indeed, if the work of a ministry team in outreach prospers, it can even model a larger shift in how the church does business — fewer official ad-ministrative boards imagining they are there to oversee others doing ministry, more engaged gatherings of people diving into the front lines of people actually doing ministry. Imagine the creativity of a church busy with ministry instead of the teapot-tempests of institutional territoriality! Dynamic, grass roots outreach sets a tone for the rest of the church.

- Reinvent how the church staff relates to the plurality of mission teams leading the congregation outside itself and beyond its recent history in ministry. Instead of expediting the flow of paper or insuring the redundancy in communications, perhaps the leader working with these teams should be more like a mentor/spiritual guide or a possibility-thinker or a travel agent. Staff could actually find it fun and dynamic to connect the unique gifts of groups and individuals with gaping opportunities to serve awaiting a Christ-like response. Institutionalism is a hard habit to break. Unless we have someone in authority to adventurously empower us to color outside the lines of how we have done business in mission over the past couple of centuries, we will miss too many exciting opportunities.

- Empower the church school, vacation bible school, and youth group to involve one-third of their curricula and activity with forms of outreach through partners like Heifer Project International, Church World Service, Blanket Sunday, Habitat for Humanity, and of course local benevolences, mostly but not exclusively Christian. These children and young people will never be more excited about coming to church — and bringing their parents — than on these Sundays. Kids have not lost their idealism about what God can accomplish through their lives and the church's reason for being. They are a real tonic for the rest of us and they keep us honest. We can always depend on our children to take the lead in changing the culture of a congregation. As Jesus quoted Isaiah, a little child shall lead us.

- Focus on local, regional and global mission partners with whom there is the chance to involve the church's people directly in the trenches of what they are doing. Let them know that direct involvement is a key criterion by which you plan to establish relationships with future mission partners. Invite them to think in creative ways about breaking down the gulf between the church and the world, and letting what they do become personal to the church's people. Focus on fewer relationships with mission partners if attention is spread too thin, so long as the relationships entail living, breathing, two-way give and take. Here, the national church can be very helpful in making such opportunities possible, such as the UCC's Back Bay Mission in Biloxi, Mississippi, and its formidable leadership in rebuilding Gulf Coast devastation.

• Let mission become the occasion for faith testimonies. As the personal experiences evolve, tell stories in worship and other settings — including both the pastor's and others'.[9] Where church people are willing to enter the trenches of direct engagement to bring compassion and healing by working directly with mission partners, those people will experience transformation. Let their light shine and do not hide it under a bushel. Let their stories establish a mood for the church and a keynote for Sunday morning. Invite people to speak freely about how they have changed, how they saw the face of Christ in the face of their neighbor, and how God is alive and at work in the world. Let the work of the body of Christ become personal through known and trusted human faces and hearts.

• Don't forget small groups in short-term mission initiatives as the basic unit of intensive transformational outreach. Take no more than fifteen adults and get out of town to some place crossing boundaries of race, creed, color, class, education, culture, language, and the like. When people get outside themselves and putting themselves in touch with neighbors like this, they throw themselves into the dilemma for which dependence upon God and one another becomes necessary, and within which faith in God makes sense of the world. Doors and windows fling open, light and air flood in. Then these people come back home to the church and create a highly infectious contagion of enthusiastic reconciliation and healing. It is the best kind of leaven in the loaf.

- Create big events that offer a larger tent which many people can enter, people who are unable to leave town on a mission trip for a week or so. This setting creates a kind of mission clearing-house and carves out a niche for mission and outreach right at the core of the congregation's life. It could be a Thanksgiving or Christmas meal for the homeless. It could be a mission trip for young people that reaches into the local public schools and community, and brings new families into the church and exposes them to the life of faith. It could be a local Habitat for Humanity home or advocacy of a holy cause that finds no root in your community or partnership with another religion in sending the message of God's radical hospitality for all of God's children. It could be locally taking up the cause of a disenfranchised group in the community, such as the national United Church of Christ did in identifying the many sites where toxic waste dumps were situated in proximity and peril to the poorest of our nation.

The heart of mission and outreach is personal and faith-filled, not institutional interaction of one agency talking to another well-meaning bureaucracy, losing the individual entirely along the way. The essence of mission means getting people involved and immersed in the streets and byways where the reign of God is worked out through great fear and trembling. This means the leveling of the formidable barriers to keep people apart that the secular world has erected and sanctified. Mission loses big-time when it is reduced to no more than attending meetings, reviewing last month's minutes, writing newsletter articles, allocating lump sums, and writing checks.

Mission and outreach are the adventure of sharing the common pilgrimage where the Holy Spirit would lead us. And that will always be to some very surprising places that we could never have reached without God. Mission and outreach are about seeing the face of Jesus Christ in faces we otherwise never would have seen, just as he invited us to do so. As we accept his invitation, we come to know blessings that define our faith and make the church truly feel like the church. The biggest threat to this is the worship of idols like the status quo — "But we've never done it that way before!" — and security — "Will that be covered by our liability insurance? If not, we can't consider it."

Remembering God's People as Movement

Historically, the church has functioned at once as parish, congregation, and movement.[10] The parish aspect of our life is how we have related to our neighborhood and community and the special privileges we have enjoyed within these realms. Our role as parishes has been seriously compromised by the end of Christendom with society's adamant assertion of its secular nature. The congregational aspect of our life is our gathering as the worshipping and serving body of God's people. This remains at the center of our life though the surrounding environment feels forever changed. We still gather for worship, even if older forms lack the same vitality. We still configure ourselves for service, even if fewer and fewer will sign on for our boards and committees.

This brings us to that third part of being the people of God, which is movement. Movement such as Jesus ranging around the hills of Galilee with his followers; movement such as helping an indigent Native American church in South Dakota rebuild when its roof caves in from the snow; movement such as an ophthalmologist and his cohort venturing to El Salvador to treat the vision needs of more than 4,000 people in two weeks.[11] If the parish aspect of our life together as church is diminishing or gone and the congregational aspect of that life is more uncertain or even deeply compromised, the movement aspect is where we make up the deficit. That we are also a movement of God's people across two millennia is something to be remembered and celebrated, especially now. Movement is the least institutional aspect of our common life in Christ.

Movement carries with it a winning sense of adventure and possibility. It frees us from feeling like we must stifle ourselves with bureaucracy in order to think of ourselves as responsible. Movement reminds us that, when Jesus announced the coming of the kingdom of God, almost no one then or since has seriously believed that this could ever be captured by any one institution — even the church — fallible as they all eventually are. This is why, in his colorful paraphrases of the New Testament, peanut farmer and New Testament scholar Clarence Jordan always translated "kingdom of God" as "God-movement."[12] Movement helps church officers remember that our members are less like a Roman column of soldiers marching inexorably, uniformly, and unquestioningly toward conquest, and more like a rag-tag guerrilla team of recruits launching our periodic counter-insurgencies of grace once we have returned to the front lines, after first getting the harvest in to feed our family.

Movement helps the church feel like it is alive and has a pulse, just when the rest of the world would write us off. Movement involves getting outside ourselves, our deeply entrenched ways of life, and our assumptions about how things must be, clearing the way for an honest exchange of spiritual gifts where all parties on all sides always have more than enough gifts to give and receive in faith. Movement implies transformation during our faith pilgrimage, where no one expects that we will be the same at our destination as we were at our departure. Movement is the self-image the church desperately needs to reclaim to be faithful in mission and outreach at this moment in our history. God willing, that will spread to other parts of our common life — worship, education, fellowship, and the rest — to catalyze our long-awaited renewal.

Above all, imagining the church as movement is deeply personal. For movements — like the civil rights movement — are ignited by intimate encounters and not impersonal forces, like Dr. King in his kitchen feeling the Holy Spirit alight upon him. Movements — such as the rising to resist violent hatred — are empowered more by the personal memoirs of a Jewish girl named Anne Frank living her wartime adolescent struggles in a Dutch attic than by all of the cold hard facts about how many millions were marched off to the gas chambers. Because God is a personal God and the Spirit of God moves in exceedingly personal ways, we must remember that our power is that of a movement and not located in some downtown high rise of a national church.

Mission and outreach begin with something as personal as seeing the face of Jesus in the face of another human being in need, and then responding to that face. Jesus made it personal by asking precisely this of us. In moments like this we find our willingness to try to live for a moment inside that person's skin, even if it is of a color or shape unlike our own. It is daunting to think of saving a world in such terrible shape as this one, so daunting that we can only hold the thought for a moment or two before desperately needing to move on to something else.

But as we look in our neighbor's face and see the face of Christ, it becomes undeniable: There can be no real peace, no real prosperity and no real joy for us until there is peace, prosperity, and joy enough for everyone. And in that moment, instead of feeling like we must do everything alone by ourselves and then recoiling, retreating, and hiding within our excuses, we feel the urge to do something somewhere, anywhere.

We board a bus and sit down where a racist society says our kind cannot, mindful of the faces of aunts and uncles who were kept from relieving the burden on their feet. We take into our home for a while a Jewish refugee from Russia because a Jewish girl from the Netherlands touched our heart 40 years ago. We build a house for a family we will never meet in places we can barely pronounce when we are up to our eyes in mortgages because we served dinner to the homeless one year at Thanksgiving. This impulse is personal, or it is nothing at all.

It is deeply ironic, but compassion is wildly popular, and not just within the church either. When we act in compassion the church feels like the body of Christ, and even nonbelievers feel like children of God. This is no accident, mirage, or coincidence. Rather, it is rubbing up against a powerful reality of which we are too seldom aware, the reconciliation between heaven and earth that God has already begun and which will surely find its consummation. The problem is that compassion must find a human face to become real to us individually and a force among us collectively. And it does no one any good to romanticize compassion, because painfully little gets put toward this higher heavenly reconciliation simply with vast storehouses of food, righteous indignation, or good will, in and of themselves. After many decades of blessed good fortune here in America, we have learned that many times over.

Yes, compassion is wildly popular, but it is not easy to be compassionate. "The paradox indeed," Father Henri Nouwen observes, is "that the beginning of healing is in solidarity with pain. In our solution-oriented society it is more important than ever to realize that *wanting to alleviate pain without sharing it* is like wanting to save a child from a burning house without the risk of being hurt."[13]

This is why God has given the church to the world: to show the way where none now exists, to create a space of hope where walls have closed in, to allow the Holy Spirit to enlarge the possibility for action toward our dreamiest and loftiest hopes. This is why God has given the church Jesus Christ: to give compassion a human face, a face we cannot turn away from if we truly desire to become the people God intends us to be, if we truly desire to have our own part as builders in God's reign. Becoming such a people is a deeply personal act, beginning with searching our own hearts for our calling outward, and moving forward from that place until we meet God in ways and places that hardly seemed possible when we first obeyed that voice's quiet summons. The result is powerful transformation: ours and the world's. Jesus came for this.

Four

Think Big, Start Small

How much money must you have in hand before responsibly beginning to **build a new Habitat for Humanity home?"** came the question from the floor. The asker was the sturdy type, serving perhaps on his local church's Board of Finance. The question followed Millard Fuller's moving testimony in Springfield, Illinois, mentioned in Chapter One, to which we had dragged our youth group all that way and then could hardly get them to stop enthusing about on the way home.

"That is an excellent question," smiled Fuller. "Thanks for asking it. You're right. We must have something up front. I believe it would be highly irresponsible to begin any Habitat home with less than . . . one dollar in hand. Someone needs to ante up that first dollar. Never start any home without it. That would be irresponsible. Then again, if we expect large bankrolls up front and having all of these houses paid for in advance of launching construction, where's the faith there? Pagans can do that. We're Christians. We are different. We base our work upon faith. We build houses for the glory of God."

The man carefully rephrased his query as though Fuller had failed to take his point. He couldn't conceive of approaching home building, even for the poor, in a way other than everyone has learned at the feet of mortgage bankers. But Fuller redoubled his intensity and seized yet another opportunity to bore deeply down into how the economics of Jesus and our responsibility as Christians radically differ from how Chase Manhattan defines economics and responsibility.

Fuller knew whereof he spoke. He founded Habitat for Humanity in 1976 with the declared goal of eliminating poverty housing from the face of the earth. This is what wise planners and consultants call a B.H.A.G., a big hairy audacious goal. After that bold prediction, it took Habitat a full year to build even one home in Georgia. It was certainly not a rate of progress that would inspire optimism among prognosticators. Still, by building on faith with the economics of Jesus, things have picked up since then. Habitat for Humanity has built more than a quarter of a million homes for God's people in need across the face of the earth. And as all of those many interest-free mortgages come back from Habitat homeowners into their so-called Fund for Humanity; they will continue to build exponentially more homes.

These origins illustrate the theme of this chapter on Christian mission and outreach: think big, start small. This message is worth highlighting because as Christians we are tempted to do precisely the opposite: think too small and start too big. One reason the Great Society initiatives of the 1960s failed was because, after thinking big, they didn't know how to start small. After all, they were armed with tax dollars from Congress. Attacking urban poverty, for example, a full-tiered staff was hired from executives to secretaries, and office space was leased, fully-equipped with an array of office machinery — all this before the vision had been clarified and refined. There they were, all dressed up with no place to go, all of the budget going to infrastructure with nothing left over to execute the mission, no one completely understanding the mission or at least the particulars along the way.

At our best, the church is lighter on its feet than this. We are leaner, meaner, and more adroit, creatively making something out of nothing, called and inspired by a small voice, to the amazement of onlookers unfamiliar with the works of our God. At our worst, submitting to the temptation to start big, we veer from the course Jesus walked before us. We get hung up and bogged down, getting ahead of ourselves.

On the first count —think big — it has not yet dawned on us how powerfully transformative our efforts might be, based as they are in the Christian church, a community spanning the whole earth and blessed by the miracles of the God who commissioned us. Why think big? Because at Easter God has already won the centuries-old war against evil, darkness, and death. It doesn't get any bigger than that. All that remains is for us to carry forward and live out this victorious news in the trenches of need at the front lines of struggle. Looking to the church as the basic unit of eliminating poverty housing from the face of the earth, knowing that even a little sincere faith can occasion great miracles, Habitat for Humanity neither set its sights too low nor expected too much too soon. Neither should we.

On the second count — start small — neither are we aware how humbly God expects us to begin, to serve, and to wait patiently before blessing us with grander horizons, obvious rewards, and the respect of outward recognition. The coming of the day of the Lord is sure, but it is not yet here. Remember, no matter what we hope to accomplish, all of this is still about faith, about trusting and abiding in the goodness of God's plans for all of the earth. As we scan the Gospels, almost never do we see ostentatious miracles occasioning great faith. Instead, we see smallish acts of faith occasioning the great miracles. In a word, if we are too full of ourselves to pause first and begin in humble, difficult, demanding, and lowly places, neither should we expect that large miracles will be forthcoming.

Remember, this is a God who claims that the person who is first found faithful in little things will also be found faithful in greater things; it is both necessary and required that we prove our intentions.[1] Often at the beginning of our initiative outward toward our neighbors for the cause of Christ, things can seem modest and uneventful for a long, long time. Then, mysteriously, without owing to anything that we have changed or done, they take off. Do we have the patience to slowly put the pieces into place and await the time-table of the Holy Spirit? God is finding out how invested we are as tried and true servants in the reign of God. Are we merely slumming? Or are we willing to descend to be alongside those precious, blessed, and beloved in God's sight in a way that is authentic?

It is not just the neighbors to whom we reach out who first question our authenticity. "Do they really care about us? Is their desire on our behalf sincere? Are their motives right or is this merely for show and are we being used?" God, too, wants to know the answer to these questions. In speaking about ministry, specifically about the money around ministry, Jesus in his parables reminded us that we who are found faithful in little will be found worthy in much. Also, let us not forget that when Jesus talked about the transformation of the earth into a place where God reigns, he typically used images as small, routine, and insignificant as tiny mustard seeds, everyday salt, and nearly invisible yeast. That was not mere coincidence. It was by design and by example.

Think Big

"Make no little plans," wrote nineteenth century architect Daniel Burnham. "They have no magic to stir humanity's blood and probably themselves will not be realized. Make big plans; aim high in hope and work. . . Remember that our sons and daughters are going to do things that will stagger us. Let your watchword be order and your beacon, beauty. Think big."[2] Burnham ended up designing the 1893 Chicago World's Fair, New York's Flatiron Building, and Union Station in Washington, D. C.

Stuck as we mainline churches are in the narrative of decline, this might no longer occur to us. One look at a city skyline, seeing our steeples dwarfed by the rising glass towers of commerce, shows how the profile of the church has been eclipsed. One look at the giant silver screen, the expansions of regional medical centers, and biotechnological entrepreneurship shows how thinking big has rather become the provenance of secular forces, Gregory Jones reminds us.[3] Too often we equate faithfulness with the mediocre efforts that necessarily result in slim proportions for godly dreams that by every right should be more expansive. Certainly no modest cup of cool water given for the thirsty goes unnoticed by God. Certainly we do not need fanfare and hoopla to validate even the smallest kindness that we do in the name of Jesus Christ. But let us not forget that it wasn't so long ago that our forebears in faith were founding colleges and universities, hospitals and children's homes, cathedrals and symphonies.

When I was a part-time parish associate at the First Congregational Church of Branford, Connecticut, during my divinity school days, I came in late to a big idea that had found a small beginning. Senior Minister Roger Manners and the lay leadership of that church had gotten wind of a movement in Great Britain called hospice. And they were doing everything within their power to make certain that the dying within our country could have afforded to them the same comforts, dignity, and considerations that hospice mercifully makes possible. That red-brick tall-steeple United Church of Christ on the green and the town of Branford succeeded in gaining a foothold here stateside for the heartfelt irreplaceable ministries of hospice. A chapter was founded there and they quietly went about their healing work. This is why hospice in America is today headquartered in Branford. And it was from this epicenter that the movement (notice, a movement, not an institution) has spread across the country.

Initially, because of our ignorance of the work of hospice, this vision was met with much misunderstanding, with hospice being painted in dark shades of the self-proclaimed "mercy killer" Dr. Jack Kevorkian. Instead, hospice has become the best antitoxin to the poison of latter-day Kevorkians who believe that it is within our human purview to take on godlike proportions and decide who should live and who should die. Initially, some insisted that the work of hospice was not germane to the ministry of a local Christian church. They said that we should stick to what we know and leave the rest to the experts in the medical establishment. Of course, if the church remains silent in matters of life and death, a tremendous void will be left in the dialogue, a void most likely to be filled here in the United States with the question of where the most money is to be made.

The point is that the churchgoers, pastors and laypeople both, in this New England town had the nerve to dream that such a significant ministry of mercy as hospice might come to our shores and change everything we know about caring for human life in its latter, vulnerable stages. But they were willing to dream these dreams and consider that this void in our life as Americans could be filled by the benign force as gentle and as strong as hospice. All of this would have remained a pipe dream had the Branford leaders not been willing to spend time learning from those with experience, painstakingly create structures that might sustain a fledgling hospice in Branford, and patiently answer off-the-mark questions from uninformed persons like myself who were so painfully ignorant about hospice that we often verged upon suspicious.

Where are the other crying needs like this among God's people where we today think too small? Debt relief or clean water projects in the developing world? Where are the other opportunities for the coming together of the fortunate and the less fortunate, the reconciliation of heaven and earth, where we are now content to merely muddle through or do nothing? Preventative health-care for the most vulnerable? Protecting the retirement funds of working people? It lies within the authority of the church's call to truthfulness in Christ to make splashes in areas like these. From the smallest mustard seeds of faith, we can trust God to make a godly way where there is now no way. Pulling in the same direction, the church's many can draw upon the power of God's love, stronger than death.

This resurrection power is what Emily Dickinson had in mind when she wrote, "Truth must dazzle gradually, or every man be blind."[4] Where can we wow and dazzle for the cause of Christ, letting our lives become the building blocks in the building of God's reign? Where can we speak the message that the Gospel is not just one more set of ideas but the definitive force loosed upon the earth for permanent transformation? We don't pause enough over these questions in our day-to-day life as local churches. We don't step back to see the big picture and to envision what can and will be out of that larger context. Strangely, even if they run so deep they can also be disturbing, these are the questions that most of our members really hope the church will ask once we get beyond approving our agendas and minutes. Too often we never even get there. And if the church doesn't ask them, no one else will.

Start Small

Somewhere I have heard a story of Robert MacCauley, the head of Americares, being on a flight to Mexico City with Mother Teresa. As box dinners were being distributed to their fellow travelers, Mother Teresa asked how much the airline would donate to her charity if she returned her dinner. When she learned that amount, she soon had everyone, including the crew, returning their dinners. When the plane arrived, Mother Teresa asked the crew if she could also have the dinners (the actual food itself) to donate to the hungry poor. Then, when the airline provided the dinners, she asked if she might borrow their trucks to deliver the dinners to the hungry. "We don't break any laws," MacCauley wryly observed, "but we do break a lot of rules. And we never give in."

With this orientation, the first rule this twosome breaks is being so full of themselves and the global posture of their mission work that they are unwilling to get small within any opportunity; they dig deep into the barest openings from which they might pry more consideration for those upon whom little light shines. One might imagine that, with their many successes, MacCauley and Mother Teresa would think of themselves above having to scrounge in ways like these. Not so. Not only are they not above such smallish details, they are relentlessly vigilant around them. They know that, as Mies von der Rohe insisted, "The genius is in the details." One cannot see this unless one is willing to start small, apart from the glitz and glamour. This is why Jesus taught us that she who would be great must first be humbled.

In 1972, after a massive earthquake had leveled Managua, Nicaragua, the world's attention became riveted upon the devastation and loss of life. This was the occasion for the mission of mercy of the baseball hero Roberto Clemente, who died in a plane crash attempting to deliver food and supplies to the suffering of Central America. Agonizingly, help was slow to arrive, in part because the Nicaraguan dictator Anastazio Somoza was appropriating most of the material assistance flying into Managua and then reselling it on the black market to enrich himself personally at the expense of those he was sworn to serve. It was the worst of all possible worlds.

Two of the few remaining North American missionaries of the United Church of Christ, Gus and Sue Kuether, were stationed in San Pedro Sula, Honduras. They were monitoring this cataclysmic course of events from a distance, disturbed with the lack of immediate response to the wreckage, knowing first hand how hard these people's lives were even without such a massive natural disaster. They also knew that two large Red Cross ships were uselessly cruising back and forth up and down the Caribbean coast, chock-full of assistance but unable to transport their precious cargo to the disaster scene where it was desperately needed. Of course, back in this low-tech era, communications were not as instantaneous and clear as they are today. But Gus, a ham radio aficionado, fired up his set, and got involved in what little ways one man could. He was willing to start small.

Gus radioed the Red Cross ships to learn about the delivery plan. Their plan had fallen apart and was non-existent. He asked if he might set something up. Yes, please, came the answer. Then he called the owner of a transport company in San Pedro Sula and asked if he would donate the use of his trucks because of the extreme nature of the need. The owner agreed. Gus called the head of the truckers union and asked if they would donate drivers to move the goods overland in solidarity with the suffering Nicaraguans. The union boss agreed and drivers were lined up. From there, it was a simple matter of coordinating the docking of the ships in Puerto Cortes, the arrival of the semi-truck trailers, and the drivers firing them up. A convoy of help was now on the way, hopefully able to avoid Somoza's greedy clutches and find the broken and displaced who were suffering. [5]

Think big. Start small. This simple formula is the key to reaching out to neighbors in the name of Jesus Christ while maintaining both the expansiveness and the humility of our faith. Why then do we think so small in the impact we hope God might make through our witness? And why do we expect so much so soon by way of demonstrable outward results as a visible reward for being so virtuous? Jesus, who modeled otherwise, healing forgettable beggars and forgiving disposable thieves en route to saving the entire world, is unhappy with these trends in the church.

The legend has it that the humble St. Teresa of Avila once declared to someone her desire to build a hospital. "Well, how much money do you have to build?" he asked. "I have but three pennies in my pocket," she responded. "Three pennies are not enough to build a hospital!" "You are right," Teresa agreed. "Three pennies are not enough to build a hospital. . . But with three pennies and God, I can do anything." Think big. Start small. This is the stuff of miracles.

What shape does thinking big and starting small take in the local church? Usually, this impulse has to be translated to other questions like: What do we have the heart for just now as the people of God? What opening for faithfulness is God giving us just now in our common life? What has God laid upon us by way of Christ-like response to the world at this particular point in our pilgrimage? These questions must be asked in personal ways that fit into the ebb and flow of our lives together as communities. As leaders, it is not only required of us to bring the inspiration of good ideas for outreach. It is also laid upon us to broach these possibilities, asking in the right way, waiting for the right moment.

Asking questions like these, we simultaneously guard against selling ourselves short and compromising the possibilities around reconciliation and redemption in Christ even before the vision gets lifted, as the pragmatic tend to do. Asking questions like these, we keep from becoming so full of ourselves that we assume ancient evils will yield and dissolve to our superior intelligence; that we are powerful people with all of the answers to life's most intractable problems.

Journey Inward, Journey Outward

If we wish to understand what thinking big and starting small looks like, Washington, D.C.'s remarkable Church of the Saviour can trace the shape of how this renewal in outreach can occur. The genius of this congregation was the balance of their inward life of God and self in the church with the outward life of looking toward the needs of the greater community. They explored how deeper self-discovery in Christ taps wells of creativity that play out in resurgent energy for servanthood within the larger communities where God sends us out.

Again, in this interplay of inward and outward spiritual forces, we are reminded that mission is not narrowly defined as the token good deeds of the church added on after all the other church business is attended to. Mission is expansive and encompassing. It is dynamic and transforming. Mission is what happens as the entirety of our life in Jesus Christ cannot help but rise up and spill over into feeding the hungry, clothing the naked, healing the ill, and liberating the imprisoned. In this sense, mission is at the heart of our purpose and not some benevolent afterthought at our periphery. And if God's mission in Christ, reconciling the world to God, is not at our heart, then our outreach will always proceed in fits and starts, and be found wanting.

As for Church of the Saviour, they lifted five themes basic to launching any form of outreach.[7] Theme One is the need to develop an interior life, if we are to be people who are fully present to other human beings. Let's face it, before we can do anything significant, we must know who we are. Until we meet God in Jesus Christ, and know through him that we are first and last God's beloved children, we don't know who we are. Unregenerated in this personal, deep, and searching way, at best we can only hope to, as Walter Lippmann says, muddle into muddle. We certainly cannot hope for the kind of greatness that citizenship in God's reign makes possible.

If we are to grow inwardly in the spirit of Christ, we first must look to our most basic practices in the faith. Thankfully, new books and curricula are being written these days on the shape of our many Christian practices, which for so long have been neglected because of our overemphasis on doctrine and belief.[8] Prayer, for example, is one quiet practice where God invites us to start small while also thinking big. Great things begin as we prayerfully respond to the ordinary within a context of deep discernment and faithful discipleship around God's will for creation. Elizabeth O'Connor wrote these words, speaking on behalf of Church of the Saviour:

> There is a profound sense in which our whole life is prayer, whether we strive for it or not, so that much of what we wail and complain about is an answer to requests we are not conscious of making. If we take with any seriousness the idea that our whole life is prayer, surely we will want to meditate on what our posture, and attitudes and acts, are really petitioning. The person on an inward journey in the church come-of-age will be familiar with all forms of prayers from a simple petition and intercession to meditation and contemplation and the prayer of silence. He will take the time to experience a life that is different from his life, and to see a world that is not visible to the ordinary glance.[8]

Another essential beginning point is living with Scripture and in fellowship with those persons of faith who walk through Scripture. "If we can live with the men and women of the Old and New Covenant deeply enough to hear the Word that God addresses to them, we may come to believe that there is His Word for the journey for each of us to take... One of the ways to begin on this phase of the inward journey might be to take a book of the Bible and live with it for a year. D. T. Niles says that this is one of the practices that he is engaged in for his adult life."[9] Prayer and Bible reading are but two practices we pause over as we detail what starting small looks like.

Theme Two of the Church of the Saviour's walk is the need to discover and exercise our own gifts. For the free exercise of our spiritual gifts, those gifts must be identified and find a setting where they can blossom and flourish. This means that our churches need to make better use of spiritual gift inventories (such as are available online through the Gallup organization) that educate our people and make real how God has blessed us and is calling us in specific ways.[10] Most of our people don't even know that they are endowed with gifts from God intended to be offered freely for the reign of Christ, never mind what their own gifts happen to be. Discerning those gifts is an important beginning step if we are expecting our people to stand tall in their faith and show up as we move out into the world.

Once we employ spiritual gift inventories and help our members to locate themselves within this nexus, our churches need to develop small group ministries and working outreach teams to create contexts where these newly-recognized fledgling gifts will have the setting in which to express themselves and play themselves out in ways pleasing to God. Small group ministries and ministry teams can be formed around spiritual gifts like hospitality, prayer, Bible study, creativity, service, healing, and yes, most certainly, outreach. But until we know how God has gifted us and how those gifts can serve God — individually and collectively — we cannot expect much in offering them to our neighborhoods and to the world.

The third theme basic to any preparation for outreach is the need for discipline, without which we cannot hope to realize our potential. In the mainline church, we could easily fear that word discipline. But just as a river needs banks to bound and direct its flow — otherwise it becomes a morass of a swamp — so also creating firm boundaries within our common church life creates power that God can use for good.

These disciplines certainly should include vigilant stewardship, where we expect the financial support of everyone in the church who is able to give toward those with less. This is not a matter of privacy, not a matter of preference, not a matter of lifestyle. Even a cursory glance at the early chapters of the book of Acts shows that this is a matter of being in true community, living honestly in covenant. How often do we sense that at least half of the members of our Board of Trustees, the church's principal property and finance body, give less than half the average pledge? Not surprisingly, their role is not making the best and godliest use of the funds God has placed in our hands. For such as these, faithfulness is more like suppressing "expenses" as much as possible, mission and outreach being first in line for cuts. Church members, particularly leaders, and most especially financial leaders, need to be held accountable for how God has prospered us.

Another discipline worth mentioning is establishing baseline expectations for how we treat one another in the church. In the early church, the world saw a tightly knit community of diverse people whose common bond was Christ Jesus, and observed, "See how they love one another!" They saw this quality of oneness before the faithful ventured forth out into the world, bringing the same Gospel that already reigned in the church. Likewise, we cannot hope to venture forth into the world to bring the transforming love and truth of Christ when disturbed people within the church are allowed to run roughshod over one another, unchecked by the discipline of speaking the truth in love that every church must establish to maintain the purity and stability of its common life. Until we do this, people will not necessarily rejoice at our coming to them — they might flee.

Another vital discipline for the church is maintaining that, as Christians, God calls us to do everything differently than the world does. We do this not because we have a need to be different in order to think of ourselves as special. We do this because God's ways are not humankind's ways, as was made obvious in the life and teaching, the death and resurrection of Jesus Christ. We do this even if that means we are less "efficient" in the world's eyes and more "peculiar" in our ways. We should be prepared to say early, often, and insistently, "That might be good enough for them, and that's fine. But we are Christians. That's not who we are. We do things differently." An obvious example of this is the story that opened this chapter, where the well-intentioned man of the church could not conceive that financing a Habitat home should be based more on the Sermon on the Mount than on the latest policies of the Federal Reserve Board.

Theme Four of the church's basic preparation for outreach is the need to know ourselves. We must engage in honest self-reflection about our motives in advance of venturing into the neighborhood or the world. Do we approach our neighbors because we have a desire to be perceived by others as "good" people? Do we approach them because we pity and feel sorry for those we might help? Do we do so because we will feel guilty if we do nothing, having prospered so in our own good fortune? Do we do so because it would look good on our resume? Because we think we know more about life and living than they do, and we want to help the slower and less adept?

Or, instead, do we feel led by God to be in fellowship with others, perhaps those unlike ourselves, because God intends to serve in an exchange of spiritual and material gifts so that all of God's children might live more in line with God's intentions for the earth? Do we feel sent to others because in Jesus we have learned that we are all in this thing called life together, and no one can be left behind? Of course, we all have mixed motives in our service, and God can purify us better than any smelter can extract gold from useless rocks and rubble. But if we do not examine ourselves before going forth to serve, we can easily create as many barriers as we bring down even before we begin. And then, soured by the experience, we might never return to the vocation of outreach, wondering why "those people" are so ungrateful.

Did you ever hear the story of the woman who gave generously of her time to prepare a meal for the local homeless shelter? It helpfully probes our intentions and motives. She labored long and hard to prepare a delicious and hearty soup. Her first taker came in. She served him the soup, and stood over him as he devoured it, realizing that what she was really doing was waiting to be thanked. He recognized and realized her motives at the same moment. Looking up from a fresh slurp of soup, he grinned at her, "So it seems doin' good's a hustle, too." The woman reflected later, "It was like the slap of a Zen master." If we step out in ways like this, we are going to learn things about ourselves, not always easy or pleasant, that we cannot learn anywhere else.

As we leave our comfort zones and cross formidable social boundaries to serve our neighbor, moving to spiritual terra nova, there is so much we fail to understand. Like this woman, we do well to prepare ourselves to be humbled without feeling like failures. I know faithful servants who have devoted decades to identifying with the poor and broken, and who must still learn to laugh at themselves for the ways they are caught up short in terms of failing to "get it." As we put our pride aside, as we let ourselves become small, perhaps we create more room for the Spirit of God to be present and expand into that space which our egos would have occupied. This much is certain: Persistence despite our opaqueness in serving God's children in need will eventually win over those whom we seek to serve. For, counted as invisible nobodies in the world's scheme of things, they too surely know all about humility.

The fifth and final theme that is basic to preparation for outreach, if we are ever to cross that line where life's emphasis is more on giving than on receiving, is the need to be shepherds. We live in a time of affluence, and that God wants prosperity for us is a good thing. But we are ill-equipped to handle prosperity, as rare and unaccustomed as it has been in human history. Consequently, affluence has become "affluenza" and the extreme self-absorption of narcissism has become our primary condition. We measure everything by the yardstick of whether it stands to benefit or to please us. We spin out our dreams and devote all of our energies to pursuing these personal utopias. But none of this is real; it is all illusion. Somewhere along the line we have forgotten that God sent us Jesus precisely to proclaim God's dream, which Jesus called the kingdom of God.

Our egoism notwithstanding, we are not at the center of the universe. The real audience and evaluator of life is the author of life, the God who created and redeems us in Jesus Christ. If we pursue God's dream for humankind before seeking our utopian dreams for ourselves, the best dream we could possibly entertain comes true not only for us, but for all people. God's is not a dream in which the benefits for the few come at the expense of the many. In God's dream, no one gets left behind, and we pass beyond that mystical point to where life is not just about receiving. This is the tipping point toward the highest and holiest joy. Those of us who have lived lives lost somewhere within affluence have forgotten even that such a point exists.

If we don't know where to start in our outreach, these five themes from Church of the Saviour point us in small directions from which big dreams can gather, like the gentle beating of a butterfly's wings off the coast of East Africa welling up into global systems transforming communities thousands of miles away.

Think Big, Start Small — Epilogue

Back in the late 1980s, the St. Vincent de Paul Society of Columbus, Ohio, approached the First Congregational Church on East Broad Street and asked if we might help with their Christmas Day dinner and celebration with homeless street people. They could accommodate only two or three hundred persons, and the need was greater. Theirs was a vital ministry, they felt, and they wanted it to continue. Could we help?

It seemed like a good idea to most of us. The proposal glided through committees until it reached our Board of Trustees, who couldn't envision this happening in our church. The building is a neo-Gothic cathedral designed by John Russell Pope and listed on the National Historic Register. The vaulting in the nave rises some 65 feet above glistening floors and French stained glass windows, exposing a 3,700-pipe German pipe organ towering within the balcony. The trustees imagined the homeless milling about that elegant space, and they flinched. But the grass roots appeal of taking in such an event forced them to reconsider their position when the Mission Board challenged them to do so. The matter resolved itself as the trustees, to their credit, pledged to be hall monitors stationed all around the church, protecting that jewel from defilement, and the plans were on once again.

At the first "Bethlehem on Broad Street," some 700 people found their way to our doors. A few years later the number had exceeded 2,200 guests who came to celebrate the birth of Jesus Christ. The Christmas feast continues to this day and has become a central Ohio tradition, with the media swooping in to seize upon this event that more closely approximates the spirit of Christmas than anything happening at the local shopping malls.

The first stop was on the front lawn where a tent offering hot coffee and doughnuts awaited the guests' arrival. Then the next stop was in that magnificent sanctuary where worship began seven times that day, pausing to celebrate by praising God before making other festive stops. The entire educational wing of the church (later joined by the Methodist church across the street) was full of warm clothes, made available to provide some options for battling the wintry blasts. Counselors roamed the corridors, commissioned with the purpose of stopping and listening and caring. AT&T provided free long-distance service so that those separated from their families could attempt to reconnect at least that once in the year.

It was beyond human scale, but it was warm and personal. It was massive, but it was suffused with the reconciling light of God become flesh to dwell among us. The Borden Company, whose offices were located behind the church, donated trucks for the quantities of turkeys that it would take to feed the masses. Hundreds of volunteers and servers poured in from all directions. Perhaps best of all, this "Bethlehem on Broad Street" on Christmas Day was not an intrusion on everyone's holiday; it defined it. After years at their posts, we regularly heard from volunteers that they could not conceive of Christmas without serving in this whole-hearted and utterly exhausting way.

When we began organizing this event, we could dream of hosting an event appropriate to the high and holy Christian celebration of the festival of Christmas. But we had no idea the proportions to which it would grow by a power not of our making. We certainly never envisioned that we would feed 2,200 hungry mouths, expand to other churches, and wow the entire city.

We just wanted to throw a decent Christmas bash for the people who were most like Mary, Joseph, and Jesus — the dispossessed. It took more ground work and planning than I can begin to describe. But God multiplied our efforts and our joy in a way that we were incapable of comprehending or planning in advance. Legions of devoted laypersons lowered their gaze to the task at hand and, before we knew it, something grand and inspiring and definitive happened.

Just goes to show you: Think big, start small.

Five

Let Witness Be the Watchword

Not long ago, retired archbishop Desmond Tutu spoke in a Seattle
cathedral.[1] His hearers were clearly there to show their appreciation for
his Christian leadership and personal sacrifice in moving South Africa
away from its seemingly intractable apartheid regime. The cordial exchange
hit a bump, however, toward the beginning of Tutu's message, when he was so
bold as to gently chide those present for not bringing their Bibles with them
on that occasion. The proud people in the pews were so miffed at Tutu's suggestion that few were willing to shake his hand at the door as they departed
the cathedral.

Apparently, even after seeing him in the flesh, not many of these self-
described champions for justice, equality and human rights understood what
made the good archbishop tick. Or what made him the driving force that
turned the migration toward justice and human dignity into a reality in South
Africa or anywhere else that Christians typically are able to make an enduring
difference.

For a Christian leader like Desmond Tutu, who has invited so much transformation in the direction of God's reign, leadership is not ultimately about
using the glow of his personal celebrity to endorse enlightened institutions
until they overwhelm and convert oppressors. The glare of celebrity glow

is more media-made than God-bestowed. It is not about rallying the progressive forces of history until they all align on the "correct side of history." Plenty of despots — Hitler, Stalin, Castro — made their name as progressive agents and champions of the common people. Leadership is not about playing off the fashionably correct liberationist left side of this versus the retrograde commercial capitalistic right side of that. The history of capitalist democracies teaches that the hubris of both the left and the right as explanations of life sufficient unto themselves sets them up to fall precipitously, often, and hard. Such thin approaches to Christian leadership and romantic expectations around social change say more about the callowness of Tutu's hearers than about the winner of the Nobel Peace Prize whom they had come out to hear that night.

The greatness of Desmond Tutu is at once more spiritually-centered and straightforward; it is simple personal faith set loose to grow into massive new social possibility. We have just finished considering how thinking big on the larger horizons of world transformation must necessarily start small. It starts in places like bringing our Bibles to church, like hearing God's Word before any other human word, like trusting that Word even more than conventional wisdom, common sense, or practical advice. Here small, ordinary, and even homely personal faith rises up and takes on a transcendent life of its own, and then changes the face of the earth.

Surprisingly, as small brushfires of the Holy Spirit, such simple and far-reaching faith will spread as a Christ-like blaze by which all of God's children can warm themselves. And these brushfires will meet to become a mighty blaze, purifying the face of the earth until new tender shoots appear, we begin anew, and we become more like how God intended in creating us. For Desmond Tutu, Christian ministry and social transformation is much less about human rights advocacy or becoming a liberationist rallying point, and much more about being a simple witness to God in Jesus Christ and letting that witness compel him forward.

To sever the taproot of faith — personal faith rooted within the life of the local church by word and sacrament — from the social manifestations of its blossoms of mercy and justice is to cut a living and vital life connection. And the plant cannot live long severed from its roots. Sadly, all too often plant and roots are separated in the mission and outreach of our mainline churches. A surprising number of Christians working in denominational and para-church mission houses do not even belong to or attend the services of local churches. What's worse, they perceive no glaring incongruity in that fact, because the basics of the faith — such as shared life in community with the church — are absent from their quest. I would like to hear what Desmond Tutu would say about that.

The question this chapter asks is how we can prevent our mission and outreach from becoming one more cut flower of idealism, here today but gone tomorrow, like the heady sweet Aquarian utopias of the countercultural 1960s drying up and blowing away in the millennial wind of imperial corporate America.

The first answer lies in our rootedness. Even more important than the tangible good we do in acts of mercy and justice is pointing back through those acts to the God in Jesus Christ. The little good any of us can do within any lifetime is fleeting compared to the great good of bringing others into a living and breathing communion with God, the Source of all goodness. As wonderful as it is to feed the poor, comfort the grieving, protect the exposed, clothe the naked, advocate for the powerless, visit the imprisoned, and acknowledge all persons as made in God's image, there is something even more wonderful.

It is ushering others into the presence of the true and living God as we go, particularly when we are doing Christ-like deeds of mercy and truth that will always grab the world's attention and make it more open to God's victorious grace in Jesus Christ. Those who have attempted to be agents of the world's transformation are all too keenly aware that any good that individuals do is fleeting and reversible. Our loftiest legacies of compassion and justice can quickly and easily be turned against us, forgotten, squashed, distorted, or morphed into something worse than before we ever started. But the God in whose name we act is from everlasting to everlasting, and God's victory in Christ has already been made certain at Easter. How do we know this? The Bible told us so.

Warming the World with our Witness

Witness is the word that Christians use for this transcendent sense of priorities amid the practicalities of following Jesus while doing ministry locally and globally. It is letting everything that we say and do be a vehicle for getting across our message about who God is and what God has done in the world through his death and resurrection. Perhaps this sense of priorities is what Jesus was getting at in his last words when he sent us out into the world before ascending on high. Witness was the word with which he commissioned us: "But you will receive power when the Holy Spirit has come upon you; and you will be my witnesses in Jerusalem, in all Judea and Samaria, and to the ends of the earth."[2]

In the current collective consciousness of our churches, the word "witness" is too much associated with conservative sectarian groups accosting passersby with dreary pamphlets. In the larger scope of things, this word stems from Greek New Testament word *murturion*, cognate for the English word martyr.

Of course, who other than the martyr is more aware that even the ultimate act of offering one's life is fleeting and not enough in and of itself to save the world? But the redeeming grace of the martyr is the undying hope that her loving sacrifice, given freely and gladly without regret, might point to a different and greater world where God rules, where self-giving and non-violence rather than self-interest and coercion are the order of the day. Frankly, we need this mindset of the "witness-martyr" (certainly not "martyr complexes," as they are called) if our mission and outreach are to take on the transcendent life pointing to the place where God lives and where we might hope to dwell as well. We are called to lead with our Christian witness both within the church and without, and to worry about impressive and dramatic outcomes later or maybe not at all. We need to keep God's good news of liberation and salvation in everything that we are about radiating from the center of the Christ-event — God is present, alive, and at work in Christ reconciling the world to himself.

Put another way, the church can no longer afford blithely to throw its weight unthinkingly and uncritically behind glitzy pop Zeitgeists like the media-driven Hands Across America of the 1980s or rock-and-roll benefit concerts like Band-Aid or sending our church youth groups to telethons for the Special Olympics, all the while imagining that we are doing mission and outreach in the name of Jesus Christ. For these are cut flowers, pleasing to the eye in the moment, yes, but gone and thrown in the dust heap of tomorrow. These are not the small mustard seeds that Jesus was so fond of describing, becoming a mighty and lasting shrub, where the birds of the air come and make their nests under its nurture and protection, the unfolding of this process being the working out of God's reign.[3]

I only mention these benevolent efflorescences of popular culture because I remember being a local church pastor back in the days of those events. And I recall asking — merely asking — about their appropriateness for the support and energies of the church. That wondering aloud got me some pretty stern looks from my Mission Committee. "How could you even question our involvement?" their eyes reproached. "You call yourself a pastor and you cannot see that this is God's work?"

Sometimes we forget that Jesus wanted us to be sheep to the shepherd, not lemmings catapulting off the cliff. Sometimes we cannot see that we are in this work for the long run, and that throwing our weight behind uncertain and fizzy events can breed cynicism within church people across the decades. Let's face it, the first complaint from those who undercut Christian mission and outreach is, "That money we gave to the church never made any difference anyway and ended up getting used for other purposes." We may never make this crowd happy. But neither should we lend the sanction of the church too eagerly or too glibly, especially when so many wonderful opportunities and vehicles are in place and in need of support for Christian outreach.

Maybe I am a little slow, but I didn't hear much about God in these pop culture stabs at creating a more compassionate and just world. (Actually, using the gloss of Scripture, Michael Jackson wrote "We Are the World," envisioning the miracle of changing stones to loaves to feed the poor — an ersatz Biblical image, confusing feeding the poor with what was actually the devil's vehicle for tempting Jesus in the wilderness. Close enough? Well, no.) And yes, I did need them to connect the dots for me, because I couldn't see how we could accomplish a great good like feeding massive numbers of the hungry while leaving God on the outside looking in.

This is not to say that these one-hit-wonder pop culture attempts at outreach didn't accomplish anything; they did. Neither is there anything wrong with the church riding the ripples they create. But we in the church have been attempting to love our neighbor in ways like this for two thousand years. In the latter days of imperial Rome, Christians were feeding many thousands of people off the Roman streets daily, ending gladiatorial spectacles, and raising the tiny victims of infanticide thrown into the Tiber River. That was how the church overthrew the empire. And God is better served if we take a longer view on this work and adopt a more comprehensive approach than waiting for the glare of the media spotlight to arrive and then rush in while it burns hot for a few days before moving on to create a new sensation elsewhere.

What I was sensing in our over-eagerness to ride on the back of popular culture was a church feeling itself to be nerdy and desperately wanting to be cool, a church that will always feel odd in a popular culture if all it wants is to be just one more buddy among buddies out to save the world. The problem is that buddydom doesn't cut it; buddies always go home and forget the cause when the glare of the media spotlight turns elsewhere.

I will never forget the liberation-minded UCC pastor of the early 1980s who hailed the then-new phenomenon of break-dancing as a promising source of empowerment for poor people of color to find their way out of the ghetto. "Look at the money they are making in the entertainment industry! Consider the hope this gives them and the new chances it creates!" he marveled. Yes, sure, all fourteen of them. Yes, break-dancing, as opposed to gifts like, say, literacy or jobs or housing or sobriety or health care.

Sometimes our minds are so open that our brains fall out. Sometimes our well-meaning hearts are so sickly sweet that our teeth throb and ache, or should. Maybe we get diverted like this only because our souls first are co-opted by popular culture's shallow sugary images of spirituality and justice. And correcting this sentimentality about how to make a difference in the world is precisely why Desmond Tutu wanted his Seattle hearers to hold their Bibles. To make a deep and enduring difference for good, we need nothing less than the taproot of Christian witness, growing out of the word and sacrament of the local church. If we do not proceed in this manner, accepting no less a goal than giving the world the soul of the church, the church ends up taking on the soul of the world.

To do mission and outreach in such a way that witness is the watchword means always keeping at the forefront of our endeavor the heart of the Gospel message that has been entrusted to us. This is not easy. It asks that we move into the world out of a vaster and deeper passion than the "impulse charity" which has become the industry standard not only for glitzy media-driven outreach event, but also at the check-out counter every time we go to the supermarket to buy groceries. To keep witness at the center of our outreach requires the relentless discipline of asking a lot of questions — questions that did not originate with us. Questions we are not accustomed to asking. Questions the world will never ask for us. Questions that are not easy to answer in any definitive or lasting way.

Questions like: Where is the glory of the Gospel in this? Where does redemption by the cross become visible in what we are saying and doing? How can we ourselves sink back and become less visible while making more prominent the God who is our Savior? How do the death and resurrection of Jesus become the first and final message through our words and deeds?

And these questions lead to other questions: Where does this become more about the unstoppable advance of God's reign and less about volunteerism, progressivism, boosterism, or the ubiquitous "triumph of the human spirit"? Where can we see the face of Jesus Christ among the suffering and needy whom we approach and in one another as we venture out together? Who is the final audience for our acts? Are we doing what we are doing because others will view us as good people or because God tells us that we can do no other? Are we truly participating in God's reign or building our own little benevolent empires? The first will endure forever and the latter will turn to dust and blow away.

Christian mission and outreach are essentially Christian witness. Retaining this focus is vital. Without it, we will only muddle into muddle. For the point of mission is not that it is we who save the world by alleviating misery, responding to disasters, taking up the cause of the neglected, and allowing for development. Our efforts mean to glorify God's reign in Jesus Christ, letting those occasions be the vehicle for moving us to that place where God dwells and awaits us. It is not our place to prop up other answers to existential questions, answers like "the American dream," "pick up yourself by your own bootstraps," "the power of positive thinking," or feel-good one-world rainbow chasing. Rather, it is our place and our calling to show forth the nature of who God is by the loving testimony of what we do and give. And because our God is a great God, if we are willing to take the risk of reaching across the barriers that the world creates in order to show God's nature, people will come and know God as a result.

I have tasted this often in parish ministry, but only seldom in its purest form. I remember receiving a phone call from an African-American pastor whose charismatic church ministered out of a building that Roman Catholics had abandoned. They were situated in Columbus, Ohio's Precinct 12. I knew this precinct because I had undertaken some all-night citizen ride-a-longs with the Columbus police to get a better grasp of street life in the worst part of town, a few miles away from our church and from my own cozy suburban home. Frankly, I needed more education in such environments to speak with any authority as a downtown pastor.

One of the questions I would ask each ride-a-long policeman was, "What percent of the people here engage in criminal behavior?" The cops, some hardened and others reflective, typically estimated from two to eight percent. The vast majority of the people, even the most cynical policemen insisted, are like most of us. They are trying to get up in the morning, get to work on time, keep their noses clean, take care of their families, and make a better life. Think of that: a neighborhood where the overwhelming majority is honest and industrious, dominated by such a small percentage. Such is the case in any slum, the police insisted — unchecked evil creating disproportionate fear and filling the power void on the street.

Anyway, my brother pastor called me because he was distressed by a then-new drug phenomenon appearing on the streets, a terribly potent form of cocaine called crack. He felt as though the crack subculture was not just encroaching on his church and their common life, it was washing over them like a burst sewer pipe. It threatened children playing and people venturing on their porch to get their mail. "We are going to march in the streets to confront these powers," the pastor told me. "Would you consider joining our ranks and coming with us?" Although I had never met him before, I said yes. Then, on Sunday morning, I explained the invitation from a sister church and invited any interested worshippers to accompany me. To my delight and relief, more than a couple dozen of our First Congregational Church people showed up. We were unprepared for what followed.

Rather than merely taking attendance and starting to march, our fellow Christians drew more from the civil rights model of old, when marchers prepared themselves for police dogs and billy clubs. First, we spent a few hours in the church spiritually arming ourselves for the powers we were about to confront. We prayed, we sang, we preached, we testified, we bonded together spiritually, we became one in the Spirit long before we ventured outward. Of course I had not planned a sermon, but one emerged at their insistence, the Spirit giving me the words where I only had sighs and pangs.

Once on the street, our methods were simple. (The police, having been notified, were at a distance in case violence would erupt.) We found the most notorious crack houses in the worst neighborhoods of Columbus, formed a circle of light holding hands and candles aloft, enveloped and surrounded these houses completely, and poured out our hearts to the true and living God. We sang. We quoted Scripture. We prayed. We called and responded from one side of the circle to the other. We invoked the healing power of repentance before God and hope in Christ for all of us sinners. It wasn't like we were waving a magic wand, as though evil would easily beat a hasty retreat. But we served notice, by our gently confrontational non-violent witness in Christ, that good would not forever be shoved around by evil. The light of the candles held aloft in the darkness announced that God's goodness has the final word.

Typically, we would see frightened furtive movements behind the curtains of these crack houses. Those movements reminded me of the skittering of cockroaches in the face of a sudden light, evil fleeing and scattering. Were those in the crack houses wondering whether we were going to burn them down? We were not condemning them, but we were unmistakably staring them down and drawing a line of demarcation. Some came out and talked to us. It was impressive and even inspiring. It was powerful and holy. More than whatever good we did, the point was making a witness with sisters and brothers in Christ beset by a scourge that, unchecked, could swarm over all of us. My biggest regret, in retrospect, was not doing more to call back and follow up with our new sister church in Precinct 12. Opportunities like this forever await us.

Other Case Studies in Outreach by Witness

In 1979, Gene and Jackie Rivers moved their family into Dorchester, outside Boston, and established the Azusa Christian Community, named after the roots of Pentecostalism in America.[4] The couple took a home that had been a site of neighborhood drug activity and turned it into a church and organizing center. After evolving from a militant black Pentecostal radical activism out of their experience as undergraduates at Harvard University toward an approach centered more upon contemporary black Christian martyrs, they came to understand that "there is no crown without the cross. Most folks aren't ready to hear that."[5]

Rivers wanted Azusa Christian Community to offer holistic ministry in its setting of poverty and chaos, inviting black and Christian intellectuals to create an alternative to its materially driven and violent surroundings.

> With faith, one can see beyond discrimination and poverty to a future that has meaning. Secular agencies don't explain to you why human life is meaningful, why there is a moral difference between spitting on the ground and killing another black person. [But] the church has the moral language to resurrect hope in the face of insurmountable obstacles. The only thing that is going to keep the United States from going in the direction of resurrecting apartheid is the church. If the church doesn't do it, it's apartheid in the future. . . The bottom line is that Shaniqua needs to be brought into a church, and her child needs to be taught the basic moral teachings of the Christian tradition, which begins in Sunday School.[6]

While Rivers speaks admiringly of predecessor black activist forerunners and intends Azusa Christian Community to be an expression of that admiration, he also believes that many groups in the movement historically abandoned the very spiritual resources that might have helped sustain the vision and the work over the longer haul. Surrendering to the secularism of the surrounding culture, Rivers complains, black activists and intellectuals lost the moral and spiritual vocabulary that had sustained the social hopes of preceding generations and frittered away the potential for social change.

> Our concern in the black church should have been for integrating biblically orthodox Christian theology, social theory, and policy analysis with some programmatic organizing on the ground, with the goal in mind of rebuilding a movement[7]. . .
>
> We recognize that a community of faith that is willing to really follow the leading of the Holy Spirit can make a difference in the worst neighborhood. Dramatic change will always require dramatic sacrifice. Dramatic blessings have dramatic costs.[8]

In the 1990s, the Azusa Christian Community sponsored a plan for comprehensive community development in a neighborhood devastated by urban decline. This proposal went far beyond the usual Christian otherworldliness of pie-in-the-sky-by-and-by as it provided a plan with specific community reforms. The plan featured teams of missionaries serving as ombudsmen in court with juveniles; groups dedicated to an "adopt-a-gang" ministry; black "brotherhoods" and "sisterhoods" that modeled alternative lifestyles to tribal violence; evangelism crusades on drug corners; health centers as sites of healing; and partnerships with suburban and white churches. Azusa Christian Community is a living and breathing example that, if we are to get beneath the surface of things and make a lasting difference, the face at the center of who we are is not incidental to what we do, but absolutely essential. Azusa is not alone in this approach to reaching out to the oppressed in the name of Jesus Christ.

In Charlottesville, Virginia, just outside the environs of the University of Virginia, literally on the other side of the train tracks, there is a community development center called Abundant Life.[9] Seventy percent of the people in this area could be termed the "working poor" and the rest are unemployed. The predominately African-American and Hispanic population is housed in drab housing complexes with tarpaper roofs. These households, anchored mostly by single mothers, must deal with the drug dealers who assume their posts at nightfall, waiting for business. Rydell Payne, Abundant Life's director, explains why he moved his family of five from a leafy spacious home to a small duplex nearby. "God called, and I needed to be in a place where Jesus would make himself real." His motives were to bear witness to "the love that cements itself to the conditions and fears of the oppressed."[10]

The founder of Abundant Life was a single white woman in her early forties, Amy Sherman. Having earned a doctorate in political science, Sherman sees places like Abundant Life, through the simple showing of respect and kindness to the poor, as "a foretaste of the kingdom of God." She sees such acts as a promise of the kingdom's "awesome and glorious" fullness, a "preview of the coming attraction, the Kingdom of God in all its glory, beauty, and wholeness."[11] Obviously, without formal training in theology, Sherman could teach at any seminary and put some bloom back into the cheeks of words that we religious types bandy about like jargon.

Such work in the forgotten and neglected sections of Charlottesville must bring with it many discouragements. And one would think that suffering from chronic pain as a result of an automobile accident would hardly be her platform for addressing such intractable realities. But Sherman believes that God is continuing "to break the Kingdom into this world; He is building His Kingdom," and that the people who take part in the works of mercy and justice themselves have the benefit of these experiences of the kingdom in palpable ways.[12]

Kingdom of God theology is the sustaining heart of the difference her faith has made in the world:

> The Kingdom of God has begun; Jesus inaugurated it. It is *now*. But it is also, 'not yet'. We wait and long in our still-broken world for its full consummation. But while we wait, it is the task of the church — Christ's body — to continue to proclaim the good news of the Kingdom, and to witness to it, to serve as foretastes of it. God is continuing to break the Kingdom into this world; He is building His Kingdom. And we participate in that work and we announce it to others — we point out where it's breaking in. And we witness to it. That is, in the Church we are to be citizens of the Kingdom of God, looking different than citizens of the kingdom of this world. Inside of our churches we are to be a reflection of the coming Kingdom, and we are to be doing the work of the Kingdom — a work of justice, of love, of healing, of hope and transformation. We are called to give people foretastes of the coming Kingdom.[13]

Leaves of the Trees for the Healing of the Nations

Doing good will always be its own reward, and so it should be. And doing good will always be of God. But our motives in the good we do in most cases will define what that good means and how it resonates in the world. And our motives generally shine through us or besmirch us in ways that we cannot conceal for long, even if we want to do so. Why we do what we do is crucial. Any good will stand on its own, but our motives give it meaning, shape, and direction. They point to larger realities, if we believe in any reality greater than the individual self.

We cannot simply say, "service above self," and leave it at that, as one large national service club does. Given our human nature, "service above self" is a dangling modifier, an incomplete sentence, because if we are not ascribing the goodness of our service to God, we are probably wearing it as a sign of our own goodness, like a beautifully tailored suit that is so large it could never possibly fit.

The truth about humankind is that, every time we give something, we expect something in return, we look for something back, even if it is as intangible as the glow of "good citizen" or "righteous man" in the eyes of others. Our nature is not so neutral as to allow unfettered "service above self." Every time we give, every time we serve, every time we sacrifice, it is in someone's name — someone in whose service we live our lives, perhaps God's, perhaps our own, perhaps even darker powers. Well-intending people, meaning to do good but unwittingly answering to unrecognized demons and acting out of destructive motives, have been responsible for some of the worst things ever done. Remembering that our outreach is first a Christian witness serves as an important corrective.

For what if we were to bind every good that we could possibly ever do to the glory of God in Jesus Christ? What if every cup of cool water we gave to the thirsty, every bandage we applied to the infirm, every ray of hope that we gave to the wretchedly imprisoned, every stitch of cloth we gave to the naked, every protection we offered the persecuted, every consolation we offered the grieving, was somehow tied to the death and resurrection of Jesus Christ? That is what this chapter means to propose. That is the best way to neutralize our natural propensity for taking perfectly innocent godly acts and making them into personal immortality projects or billboards to our righteousness. Or, for that matter, commercials for our favorite brand of partisan politics. Or rebuffs of controversial issues aimed at those ideological tribes who are not of our tribe.

It is also the best way to answer the charge, when our efforts fall short or peter out, that compassion and justice are not even worth attempting. It doesn't do any good; the world will never change; in the final analysis, it doesn't make any difference. I have heard this every time I have initiated a movement or led a group in any cause which the Spirit has led me to believe is of Christ. Why bother? In most cases, those who say things like this are trying to insulate themselves from the guilt of doing nothing. They are like the rich man rationalizing why he could never reach out to Lazarus.[14]

Of course, the answer is that, on Easter, Christ has already won the final victory. This world has already been forever changed through God's decisive action at Golgotha and beyond. That was assured long ago for those who see through eyes and hear through ears of faith. We are simply attempting to bring this world in line with the true and advancing reality that has not yet fully overtaken it.

The question is not whether Christ-like acts finally do any real good or make any real difference. The question is whether we believe in Christ enough to step out and participate in his victory when all of the countervailing evidence in the war between good and evil seems to suggest that perhaps God does not ultimately have the final word over our human destiny. With our human acts of mercy and dignity, we do not mean for them to possess a finality in and of themselves. That would be arrogant, claiming too much for what lies within our power. In truth, God is the primary and permanent actor on the world stage of redemption and reconciliation, and we are merely God's instruments and agents, taking our turn in our own passing generation. By touching our neighbor in the name of Jesus we are merely choosing to enter into and participate into the grand sweep of Christ's victory rather than distance ourselves and remain non-committal about what we take to be the final consummation of history in the triumph of good. To adequately understand this, we must immerse ourselves in the world of Scripture.

Ezekiel was led to the door of the temple in Jerusalem. And he noticed, of all unlikely things in that arid landscape, that a torrent of water was issuing forth from the temple.[15] This river originated at the altar where sacrifices were made. Then the prophet was led outside the wall and saw that the water was headed eastward. He was led along this stream a thousand cubits and it was ankle-deep. Another thousand cubits and it was knee-deep. A thousand cubits farther and it was up to his waist. Farther along still, instead of dwindling, it became a river deep enough to swim in, a river so strong that it could not be traversed. Then Ezekiel was led back along the river. And as he went, he saw trees lining one side and trees lining the other. He was told that wherever the river flowed, every living creature that swarms would live and prosper.

What could such a vision mean? Ezekiel was from a part of the world where water is so scarce that it defines life. He lived in a land forever faced with drought where people forever seek enough water to live. Consequently, the people never seem to have enough to eat either. The one who leads Ezekiel through his vision informs him that the leaves of the trees that have grown up as a result of the river shall be used for the healing of the nations. Ezekiel was living among a people who, when illness struck, would put up with the malady until it went away or death came. So this vision of a stream flowing from the temple and filling the land with life-giving waters is a vision of a kind of paradise. A dreamt-of, longed-for land of water, food, and medicine. A land which most of the world has never glimpsed.

The part of the vision most worth noticing is that this paradise of abundance and healing and hope originates from the sanctuary of the people, the place of worship, the altar of God. Recovery, reconciliation, and redemption of hope for humankind unmistakably originate in God and come to us as a gift of God, and more specifically in the worship and praise of God. And we do well not to forget it, not to confuse God's healing agency with our own.

The prophet reminds us that this miraculous river of God flows across time and space and had a life of its own before we started rooting around in its banks, digging channels to supply the dried-up and abandoned with its life-giving grace. The power and beauty and abundance it creates everywhere it goes was not our creation, but remains the eternal handiwork of God. Where does it come from? Where does it go? These are holy mysteries, and they all center on our Creator and Redeemer God.

We can help direct its flow, we can carry it to those who have never tasted it before, but it is not our river. The river was not our idea, never mind that it wasn't even close to our making. We can tap into its refreshment, we can recognize that human life cannot exist apart from it, but these waters do not originate from any noble human impulse. And as we share the cooling balm of these waters, we do well not to forget the headwaters whence they sprang. We get too far afield with the beneficiaries of these heavenly waters as soon as we fail to point back toward their source — which is not in ourselves or any other human power. We could say that the permanent saving grace of knowing who stands at the source of these waters is more important than any temporary benefit we derive from the quenching of our thirst or the cleansing of our bodies or the renewal of our spirits or the healing of our brokenness.

"You shall be my witnesses," Jesus charged and commissioned us, as he sent his people out into the world to advance everything that he had begun. Witnesses, Jesus said, not saviors. Witnesses, not lobbyists. Witnesses, not jumpers onto the bandwagons of popular culture. Witnesses, not scared and isolated and paralyzed individuals so overwhelmed that we cannot fix the world or even try to make a difference. Ultimately, we leave that saving work to the only one who was equal to it — the God who was in Jesus Christ, reconciling the world to himself. And we let every iota of our being, and every word we speak and deed we offer, point back to the true source of our salvation.

Six

Long Obedience in the Same Direction

Not long ago I served a church in a highly mobile well-to-do area. For a few years we were receiving new members in bunches. Lest we receive them through the front door and quickly lose them through the back door of indifference, we made a strategic decision to assimilate these newcomers by welcoming them without delay directly into the heart of our ministry. And so, even as some of them were still figuring out what the church and the faith were all about, we invited them to serve in key areas. Pairing the newbies with veteran disciples in important places, we mostly met with success, but not always.

One woman who had been glad and eager to be part of the church was invited to serve on the Board of Deacons. She was a social worker and had a little girl in the church school. She had come to the church as a visitor long before joining and was eager to get involved. We were as honest as we could be about what was expected of her in her new role. And this church was blessed with a remarkable Board of Deacons, generating several candidates for seminary, keeping a spiritual center for the church through some painful agitations, and gladly working hard for the cause of Christ with little recognition or reward. Moreover, these Deacons had a spiritual genius for transmitting their endearing sense of selfless Christ-like service to incoming deacons across the years. They were a remarkable group in all of the right and important ways. It was an Edenic spot in the life of that church where the pastors could sigh grateful prayers as they recognized this is the way things are supposed to be in the church.

Everything in this transition of our new Deacon class seemed to be going well. But after taking her turn through months of staffing our four weekend worship services, with communion for at least two of those services, including all the preparing and cleaning up, the welcoming and the follow-up, the new deacon balked. She dropped out of sight. I telephoned her and asked if we could meet briefly. She was pleasant and bore no grudges. And she was candid about her sudden reticence and why she was leaving the church entirely.

"My time is valuable. If I were working my caseload, I would charge for all of these hours. The work here is hard and long. And I don't understand why I should offer my time for free to the church. I'm not willing to do it anymore. It's not worth it to me. It's just that simple." It was another episode in our narcissistic serial of life rubbing up against genuine self-disinterested sacrifice, at the heart of the call to discipleship, only to turn heel and uncomprehendingly walk away.

More than anything it reminded me of the story of Jesus' encounter of the rich ruler. The spirit in which she so glibly walked away — as though the Gospel just wasn't worth it, as though her own time, gifts, and life were worth more — was what spooked me the most. It was a parting, just as Luke describes it. Yes, each party continued on, but with great sadness because it felt like a spiritual death of some kind. And as the other Deacons heard of the manner in which this woman had left, it depressed them too, for the spirit in which she responded to her opportunity to serve was so inimical to the spirit in which they gladly offered themselves and grew in their faith.

Mission and Outreach within a Spiritual Marketplace

Ask the elder members in our churches about the spiritual life of their adult children, and they will talk about them dabbling in Scientology and Eckankar, Wicca groups and Native American spirituality blogs, Eastern religions and New Age feminist writings. They will quote their progeny as describing their search for the sacred and their flight into these "spiritualities." Ask those same parents who those religious bodies are or what these things mean, and they will scratch their heads. Ask pastors you know about the books that parishioners give them, and they will reply that they are mostly self-help books, often with commendations like, "This book saved my life. I can't believe those that are doing ministry yet haven't read it."

If the church has somehow lost the gravitational pull of its power of attraction, people have not lost their fascination with things spiritual and religious. What is different today is how many of them revolve around the self instead of God. Or, as someone once said, the problem with people who stop believing in God (or at least the God in Jesus Christ we call upon) is not that they believe in nothing, it is that they believe in everything. And the degree to which we strain to "believe in ourselves" is inversely proportional to our willingness to believe in God.

The majoritarian faith of our day has been described as "cafeteria religion." What this means is that is each person is encouraged to put together an individual menu of meaning from a copious religious smorgasbord — scraps from cross-cultural myths, stress-controlling meditative practices, esoteric speculations, aphorisms from Eastern religions, and a bit of mysticism perhaps based in physics. This is the religious environment within which we find ourselves.

It means that religion today is taken as fundamentally a private matter, more a function of individual preference in the moment than the practices and traditions rising out of a community across millennia; sacred texts are all over the place, not found in one book. In this environment, ethical claims are utilitarian ("what works for me") and often devised on the spot based on who gets hurt the least. It also means that one's spirituality is measured by benefits foreseen and accrued, not by those sacrifices for which we would give our lives.

It is this last point — sacrifice — that is most salient in this chapter as we consider our platform for mission and outreach as well as the nature of our appeal to the church and to the world. If even our religious impulse as modern people has itself yielded to a culture of narcissism, then sacrifice is decidedly out of fashion. And we don't have to look far or long to confirm that this is in fact the case. Still, it is impossible for us to become ennobled, to become the person God created to us be, if we are rendered incapable of living for anything higher than ourselves, if we have forgotten the God in whose image we were formed and who holds our destiny in his hands at the end point of history.

So we can neither avoid nor soft-pedal the place of sacrifice at the heart of the call of the Gospel out into the world. At some point, we are going to have to break this news to the self-absorbed for whom it has become anathema. And there is no other way to say it than simply to let it fly. But how does this decidedly unpopular and against-the-grain-of-the-times invitation get mediated in the church and the world? Certainly this challenge is more profound than finding the right way to "market" or pitch the invitation to follow Christ. Indeed, the whole notion of marketing here is more part of the problem — the relentless appeal to self-interest — than part of the reversal in direction we seek in the environment of "affluenza." Here is one small example of how I have seen that turn.

In her prosperous high school, my daughter Lise's friends typically spent their spring breaks basking in places like the Turks and Caicos Islands or Grand Bahama Island for spring break. On the day before lighting out for these glamorous destinations, these privileged young mocked Lise for spending her spring break with me and a dozen other church members. We were off to Central America to root around in the dirt, bruise our shins, and inexpertly but earnestly build homes alongside those who barely had outhouses. After a week of not always efficient hard labor, we could see walls rising out of the ground for two snug little Habitat for Humanity homes. The criticism Lise's glamorous friends levied came from the same spirit that moved our short-lived deacon: Why in the world would you want to do that for others, when instead you could be doing this for yourself? What kind of crazy and stupid is that?

And yet over the years, by osmosis through Christian community, Lise had been initiated into Gospel mysteries — mysteries like whoever would save her life would lose it, but whoever would lose her life would save it, mysteries that never made any sense to that deacon. Because of this, as our mission trip ended, Lise defiantly asserted that she did better by sweating six days in the dust with strangers she will likely never meet again than did her friends by swimming in coconut oil and room service. Of course, it didn't hurt that we grabbed a short afternoon of relaxation at a gorgeous Pacific compound in El Salvador offered by friends of friends. That brief moment in the sun meant a lot to her, as it did to all of us. But in Lise's lasting and memorable time at the front lines of God's reign, she believed that she had tasted the best of both worlds. She tasted what Jesus intended for us when he told us to seek first the kingdom of God, and these other beautiful things that God wants for us will be added or given to us. She liked the taste, and I hope she never loses it.

No Apologies, No Excuses, No Embarrassment

One of the biggest and most dynamic churches in the United Church of Christ did not get to be that way by theological half-measures and deep compromise in ministry. Chicago's Trinity United Church of Christ, described in Chapter One, adopted a motto long before they numbered in the thousands: "Unashamedly Black, Unapologetically Christian." Dr. Jeremiah Wright and his cadre of leadership have built a remarkable ministry reaching out far and wide, producing the likes of Barack Obama, because they are unafraid to expect a lot from their people and refuse to round off the sharp edges of the demands of the Gospel. For example, in finding leaders, they don't say to their own, as many of our nominating committees say to our members, "Oh, there's not much to that job, you really don't have to do anything. You can do as little or much as you want."

What if all of our churches were unapologetically Christian (even if we are not all so blessed as to be unashamedly black)? The point here — the central point of this chapter — is that we cannot pretend that truly extraordinary things will not be required of us if we are actually following a Messiah who died for the whole world and was resurrected to affirm and underscore his role as our Savior. We cannot act like business as usual if we are living out the latter end of the greatest story ever told, the story of God redeeming and reconciling the earth before the coming of Christ. And how extraordinary is that, when all is said and done? A quick survey of the most alive and dynamic churches in America today shows congregations who are not embarrassed or apologetic about actually expecting something from people who enter their doorways — indeed, often expecting a lot. Sacrifice for God is not evaded or sugar-coated but exalted.

As we stage our mission and outreach we are called to do so joyfully and invitingly. And what is the nature of our Christian joy and the substance of our invitation? It originates in the self-giving love of Jesus and is pointed directly at that hole in that heart of modernity known as sacrifice. Giving ourselves up and giving ourselves over for what God in Christ has deemed essential is anathema to our narcissism. It smokes us out of our vacuous affluence. It fills that hole in our heart.

We live in a time and place that is rich in things but poor in soul, as the hymn "God of Grace and God of Glory" reminds us. Our calling as the church is to open the way to spiritual riches yet untapped. Ironically, those riches are located in some of the poorest places, poor as the Beatitudes proclaim, among broken, forsaken, and uncelebrated people. As Christians, we already know that the most powerfully transforming self-transcendence anyone could experience is to enter the struggles, the causes, and the tragedies where God's heart is most heavily invested. If we have any doubts about where God has left his heart hanging, a quick stroll through the Sermon on the Mount will serve nicely as our refresher course.

As we proclaim this appeal for serving God, as we issue this invitation to the world on Jesus' behalf, we do so better if we eschew a strident, demanding ethical insistence. As non-committal as mainline churches can be about personal morality, we can also be positively militant in public pronouncements on equality and justice. Our invitations to serve God in the world can take on that same stridency.

We do better if we lead in personal ways, with the radiance of our own spiritual discovery showing itself as we are led out of ourselves and among the people where the reign of God quietly and unobtrusively unfolds. We do better if we tell the stories of what happened and if we witness (there's that word again) about how this has changed us and how God promises it will transform the world. In a word, we do better if we model what we are talking about rather than squawking about it, if we create a contagion of grace instead of trying to inoculate political environments of all wrong on our way to spiritual utopias. As rare as it is to find joy in sacrifice within a self-seeking world, that amazing fact will be noticed.

Like Lise, none of us knew what Jesus means by saying "whoever would save his life will lose it, and whoever would lose his life will save it," until someone showed us. In all likelihood, someone else modeled this Gospel as a countercultural alternative to the reigning culture, obeyed a holy impulse and forgot themselves for a moment, or demonstrated a frontier for adventure that was mostly abandoned and forgotten. We are not logically persuaded into the Gospel mysteries so much as we are initiated into them little by little, letting go of ourselves to allow God room enough to take hold of us and make a difference.

The sacred mystery of self-transcendence by yielding and emptying ourselves before God is not so much explained in words as it is revealed by the radiance of spiritual discovery. And that discovery is ineffable, as often as not defying our attempts to capture it with inviting and challenging words. So our question becomes how to invite people to break through the many layers in our cocoons of bemused materialistic distraction and to dwell in a place of spiritual discovery? If we want to nourish within our churches the opportunity to become the eyes, ears, hands and feet of Jesus, let's remember and chart a few examples.

Radiance More than Persuasion

When I was a boy, I went to church camp on Lake Michigan. The denomination would, now and again, bring missionaries home on furlough from far-off places like Africa. And they wisely mixed those missionary children in like leaven within the loaf of the too many well-to-do suburban children at camp. The missionary children, with Chicago roots, were very much like the rest of us — children remain children everywhere — except for certain critical points where our differences became obvious. These were spiritual differences that cut quite deep.

I remember a brother and sister as camp was drawing to its August close. We knew they were headed back to Africa. No more TV. No more Dairy Queen. No more water skiing. We were sad for them, having to return to a life of hardship, surrounded by poverty we could not imagine, a life so full of sacrifices. We didn't really know how to say it, but some of the bolder ones among us just blurted out our regret their salad days on furlough would soon end, and they would have to return to their hardscrabble life with such grindingly poor people.

When those missionary children heard of our regret on their behalf, they were befuddled, taken aback. They didn't understand, but they did patiently explain, for they had been offered this pity before. "No, we don't eagerly count down the days before we get to come back to the United States. We eagerly count down the days before we get our lives back in Africa. We can't wait to get there!" It was their gentle way of saying, "Don't cry for us, American suburbia." They had something that we didn't know about, a life that was rich and a community where there was coherence and a sense of meaning — though impoverished by our standards, rich in other ways that teased out our spiritual imaginations.

Disneyesque America was not the land of their dreams. How could that be, we wondered. How could they not burn after the same things that we so ardently sought: BB guns, Barbie dolls, go-carts, transistor radios? Had they been brainwashed? Or, a shiver went through us — banish the thought! — maybe we were the ones co-opted and deluded somewhere along the way? Could there be a life better than that promised by the American dream? That seemed impossible. Still, there was an impasse: Either they didn't get it, or we didn't. In that moment of cognitive dissonance we were thrown into a spiritual dilemma. Even as the countercultural outbursts of the sixties were impending, we had never before considered that it was possible not to supremely want this American dream we had been sold. After all, the rest of the world wanted what we already had, yearning to make landfall at our shopping malls. Suburban American children learn that at a young age.

These missionary children were living less in a land of Disney's dreams and more in a land of God's dreams. And we were startled how this fact challenged the peace we had made with our own dreams that were grounded elsewhere than in Biblical visions. So startled, indeed, that today, decades later, I remember these children and their alternative spiritual field of reference points. It was the best possible way for our closed set of materialistic assumptions to be challenged and found wanting. No moralizing from parents. No sermonizing from pastors. No lectures about starving children in India being happy with the food we found unpalatable. Just their simple embodiment and clear radiance of a whole other freedom and happiness that had nothing to do with gross national product and everything to do with God. Best of all, it was unscripted, unprompted, unrehearsed, and entirely spontaneous.

It is possible to set up these same grace-filled confrontations in worldviews — God's and ours — today. But so often they seem to happen by stealth, by the same kind of clever indirection that Jesus employed with his parables, by astonishing discovery in moments we least expect them, moments when we are found vulnerable and unprotected against what God is doing in the world.

Can this be programmed? Not always. But it can be occasioned if only we have discovered something like what the missionary children had discovered, only if we have tasted the richness of God's dreams and come to prefer them to human dreams. And only if we are willing to invite others into the radiance of our discovery. In the final analysis, it is much like the message on the card that John Wesley placed squarely in pulpits before he began preaching: God has set me on fire so that others might see me burn. How can we communicate burning and hungering and thirsting for the ultimate righteousness of God's reign upon earth?

Creating a Contagion of the Richness of Life Lived Loving our Neighbor

It is daunting how many paths we could travel as we invite our churches into the mystery of saving our lives through losing them to what Christ lived for and exemplified through his death and resurrection. For example, the United Church of Christ, through its predecessor bodies, has been a leader in Christian mission and outreach for centuries, including distinguishing itself with organizing around the rebuilding of New Orleans and the Gulf Coast after Hurricane Katrina. The UCC and other denominations offer many other worthwhile Spirit-led impulses. Beyond the denominations, worthy para-church Christian bodies abound — some local and others worldwide — working in areas like housing, medicine, advocacy for political prisoners, clean water, community organizing, support of job cooperatives, on and on. These are all inviting resources. Ecumenical church groups ranging from local area church councils to the World Council of Churches respond to the crises of human need by creating opportunity for Christian witness and service. Their pan-Christian perspective is expansive and embracing.

My counsel amid all this choice? Begin where your heart is, where you can become a burning bush in a dark lonely night, burning in desert wildernesses of spirit, burning hot but never consumed. Begin where you can burn in such a way that the voice of Yahweh can be heard clearly through your best efforts. Actually, more precisely, begin within the heart of God, the heart of where God would send you and those whose lives God would have you touch. The dreams of our own hearts are finite and filled with our own glory, but the dreams of God's heart reveal the expansive greater divine glory, embracing all and leaving no one behind. Begin in God's heart as a matter of spiritual discernment, where both individual and community have their own say about the promptings of the Holy Spirit in their own season, about where a particular church might be led at a given moment in time. And don't be surprised if that gets couched in ways that are personal and even idiosyncratic.

In my case, that has meant a focus upon Habitat for Humanity and the yearning of the poor for a simple, safe, decent place to live. In addition to the handful of homes that churches I have served have built in Ohio, Colorado, and Connecticut, these churches have also built homes in Central America and the Caribbean. How did it turn out for me to go this way through Habitat? It was, as is so often the case, a combination of reasons through my own winding story.

Why is my heart located in this place? Because of my family's mission background in Latin America going back over fifty years, I learned Spanish with the avowed goal of visiting my aunt and uncle's mission in Mexico. This helped me enter into a more direct and explicit dialogue with people in these parts. Also, the historic presence of the UCC's predecessor churches was weak in Latin America, and so I couldn't get there through my denomination. Finally, during a post-college trip from the north end to the bottom tip of South America, my best friend and I nearly lost our lives after a coup d'état in

Argentina after being arrested at gunpoint and taken to a barbed-wired federal penitentiary. We were allowed to leave only because we were white, spoke Spanish, held American passports, and would have been more trouble than we were worth to the Argentine military in a wave of terror where 30,000 people eventually perished.

After such an experience, most vacationers would exclaim, "By God, I'm never going back there again!" But the Christian reaction might be very different: I will return as an ambassador for Christ to be alongside those who are not white, who don't hold American passports, and to whom the military would not even consider listening to from the discard heap of a federal penitentiary. Callings are found in places like these for those who have eyes of faith to see and ears of faith to hear. And we need not go to places as exotic as South America to discover them. As columnist Ann Landers once observed, most opportunities are missed because they come disguised as problems.

I tell my story not because it is either remarkable or unique. Anyone who spends enough time in the developing world at all close to the people will be thrust into a circumstance like this. I tell it to evoke within you, the reader, your own story. Where is God speaking to you and sending you out of the narrative of your own life? Who are those you know who lack voice or recourse, to whose side God is calling you? Where is God sending you in a way that would take you outside of yourself, beyond your comfort zone?

It doesn't have to be overseas; it could be a city or a neighborhood, a newly depressed farm prairie, a few states or counties away or next door. Why not seize the opportunities at hand to cross barriers of race, class, color, religion, language, geography, sexual orientation, and culture — barriers that the world uses to keep us going after each other's throats? These opportunities are too easy to miss, as intimidating as they are. But as God sends us into the breach, we are not sent alone.

Near Backyards or Far Horizons?

Some say charity begins at home, and that mission and outreach should begin with our immediate environs and neighbors. After all, God helps those who help themselves, right? Of course, these are entirely non-biblical and often self-serving sentiments. But if these sentiments mobilize you and others and get you out into the routine of your lives and out into the struggles of the broken and forgotten, then God can redeem even these commonsensical little paganisms.

At the same time, we should recognize that "charity begins at home" means something completely different if you live in New Orleans or in the South Bronx or in the Cass Corridor of Detroit than if you live in Greenwich or Palo Alto or Winnetka or Cherry Creek. In the latter category, which encompasses a disproportionate number of prosperous church neighborhoods, we probably need to make a break with our immediate environment as a dose of cold water in our face to open our eyes to how much work needs to be done and how dramatic is the need out there. In so many of our churches, we have no idea what life is like for a wide majority of people in the world. Life in the American empire tends to insulate us from those realities, and this is not a time for softening the lines of these barriers set up between peoples.

I have found that organizing a core group of a dozen or so and putting some distance between us and our home turf sets up a more intense and powerful dynamic for transformation. It dramatizes both the need of the people we are going to and our own deep need in going. If you are working with youth, take them out of their comfort zone, make them utterly dependent upon God and one another, by putting a couple of states between them and their cozy bedrooms. Places like Heifer Project International ranches in South Dakota and Winnebago Native American mission churches in Wisconsin and the elderly in the hill country of impoverished Kentucky and the struggling jobless of Maine — all places that I have been blessed to travel to with youth — will become the backdrop for the playing out of a spiritual drama that is impossible in our familiar shopping mall backyards.

If you are working with adults, you can be more adventurous still, traveling to lands outside America to break down our assumptions about the poor and their lives and to break loose our sense of what God is making possible today out in the world. The $80,000 Habitat for Humanity home that we built for a deserving family in Connecticut could have built maybe eighteen homes for a whole community in central Honduras. And, of course, the conditions of poverty in Honduras — for many families, not even an outhouse — are even more excruciating than what we find here in America. This is not to favor one over the other; it is to assert that we need to do both. In a shrinking world, Jesus' command to love our neighbor expands and takes on new dimensions. And the overriding sentiment will always tip initially for beginning close to home.

But as you travel to foreign lands or distant states with a core group of disciples bent on asking what God is doing in the world and your lives, more often it is possible to create something like a Spirit-infused contagion which has power to transform the entire congregation upon your return. This dynamic is not unlike that which Jesus seized upon in calling twelve men away from their jobs and families, their routines and familiar environs. Small groups of deeply changed people, people who "get it" because of deep immersion in the possibilities for God's reign, people who have glimpsed this reign and developed a burning hunger to spread it — that was what Jesus saw as the best place for a beginning point toward holy headway in staking an outpost for God's reign.

And it is what I see as the best opening to call, mobilize, and deploy people today. This is how we get mission and outreach (and maybe also the occasional fairly benign microbe) into the bloodstream of the church. The contrasts that we will experience with this approach are more dramatic and do not allow us to forget as easily as, say, what we did locally last Saturday for a few hours. This approach, taking a small group out of its comfort zone, has a better chance of sparking something like a conversion that is shaken off less easily.

After a few of these Habitat for Humanity trips abroad from a Colorado church, the impassioned church foot soldiers bought seven acres of Colorado soil through the local Habitat affiliate and filled those acres with homes built by this and other churches, the town university, a women's guild, and others. I am not sure that this local blossoming of grace would have resulted without that start: getting way outside ourselves first in Guatemala and Mexico. Initially, when I had asked that church about going abroad, the response was a flat no. But we went anyway. Numbers and enthusiasm swelled with each trip. After I left that church to serve another, they were placing brass plaques on the wall inscribed with the names of everyone who had ever gone on these trips and a colorful native Mayan weaving announced with pride our connection to that part of the world. This space marked and celebrated the new foothold that mission and outreach had gained in our church after the initial "no."

Maybe you worship or serve in a church with similarly hunkered-down instincts and where there is an initial and consistent "no" whenever you raise the possibility of staging such a trip, near or far. How do you respond? For my part, I believe that we can't be disrespectful to our people in their "no." But because Jesus himself has said such a resounding "yes," neither can we accept it as a final answer. We must approach it again and again through the stealth of worship and prayer, through the indirection of Jesus' parables, where God constantly bids us outward.

Start with a small trip — perhaps a middle school weekend work camp to the District of Columbia to work with the urban indigent in the shadows of our national monuments — and let them come back and tell their story and show their enthusiasm. If you don't have enough youth in your church, contact area churches. In all likelihood, they are just waiting for something like this to happen. Talk about setting up a contagion! Find creative and imaginative responses to the congregation's initial "no" rather than entering into a fighting confrontation against it that would only violate the spirit of what is being attempted. I have been told "no" in every church I have served — including my current one. My job is to help them say "yes." It is a calling that requires no small amount of imagination. If I leave the Holy Spirit some room to move here, though, I find that I don't have to do it all myself; it is not all up to me.

Perhaps the best way to "sell" these church-staged mission trips to the local church is to help people grasp that they are cultures for growing better disciples. And discipleship always translates in untold ways once we get home. So we lift up these trips not as do-gooder caravans for some amorphous notion of progress or self-improvement, like an expedition by Rotarians or Kiwanis or Masons. (God bless those service groups for all the difference they make, by the way!) The invitation to these mission trips need to be couched as a spiritual pilgrimage where our gifts of faith-filled discovery might well exceed whatever tangible difference we make in the housing, medical well-being, or job status of those whom we stand alongside. These trips are not about us as the strong and successful American "haves" helping the fumbling and dithering developing world "have-nots." They are not about giving them measured doses of our American success while taking no thought for ourselves.

Rather, as explained in Chapter One, these trips are about an exchange of gifts among very differently gifted people whom God brings together for a short time to awaken new possibilities within each other and the world. Our hosts are rich in time and poor in capital, for example, while we are rich in capital and poor in time. Is either better or stronger or greater than the other? Not really, they are just different. God will work through our different giftedness to open eyes on both sides about how we are all simultaneously both gifted and needy. The spirituality of how differences like these get mediated in our time together makes all of the difference in the kinds of transformations that are wrought. Discoveries like these are major landmarks on the journey of discipleship.

The important point here is that none of this will be articulated and realized unless someone theologically inclined, often but not always a pastor, is willing to interpret who we are as disciples, why we are going by way of our vocation in Christ, what such quiet and covert acts mean in a world dominated by glitz and glamour, and where we pray that it will all lead in terms of the prophetic vision of God leaving not one of God's children behind. Each of these trips needs a prayerful and reflective spiritual guide to interpret what is happening as it happens. Otherwise we will fail to hear the more powerful messages in the still small voices through which God is speaking to us.

This is the work of careful cross-cultural orientation before we go. This is the work of Bible study before, during, and after. This is the work of fundraising where our hearts begin to be convicted by the task at hand. This is the work of planning quiet-time morning watch booklets for our people before the day begins and evening devotionals that hear the quiet voice through which God speaks in tiny details as we move through our week. This is the work of celebration and story-telling in worship with the entire congregation upon our safe return. More important than the tangible results of our physical efforts — and, yes, the work does matter because it is such an equalizer between peoples — is what happens in the hopes that resurge when the mission theologian-interpreter lifts up these tender and sweet exchanges shining as the Light of the World.

This is how mission and outreach become deeply transformative ministry fraught with possibility as we return home instead of one more dose of liberal guilt, grim obligation, activist self-righteousness, or benevolent condescension toward the inept. Neglecting the essential work of providing this devotional-theological narrative of God's ongoing redemptive work will often mean that the experience will be described in less satisfying terms — such as conservatism versus liberalism — and will create a wedge rather than unity within our churches.

Stepping out like this — "just do[ing] it," as one sports company enjoins — is the single best place to begin in making a break with our culture of narcissism, our aversion to sacrifice, our fear that we will go through life without getting our fair share of whatever the world happens to be handing out at the moment. Such bold acts of stepping outside our comfort zones to walk where Jesus walks — whether local, regional, or global faith pilgrimages — blow open wide holes in our overwrought self-absorption.

These pilgrimages create their own logic, momentum, spirituality, authority, and rationale even where we have not been granted "permission" to do so by boards and committees nor "permission" to be the church in a world that has less and less room for us. They catch and sweep up and carry the congregation along paths we have been waiting too long to travel. The joyous enthusiasm they create in finally being about real solid ministry gives backbone and vibrancy to the ethos of the congregation. They remind us why God has placed the church on earth and sustained us for 2,000 years. They send all the right messages to the world by way of Gospel witness, as those who know nothing about Christianity recognize something of it in the reality of these ventures. They confront our self-love head on with divine love, and call us outside of ourselves to places where we can see the face of Jesus and the acts of God.

In this is love — not that we loved ourselves so much that others could never do enough for us, not that we tried to love each other in selfish ways and got frustrated and walked away. But that God refused to give up on us despite all of this, even unto sending Jesus, who lived his life with, counted as his friends, and ate and slept with simple and uncelebrated peoples very much like those we seek out. In this is love — not that we loved but that God loved us, gave us Jesus as the atonement for our sins, was vindicated beyond his ignominious death, and lives in the world, where this drama continues to unfold in our own day. The question congregations must be asked is whether they are ready to assume their God-appointed parts as we make this drama of redemption real by acting first and organizing elaborate structures later.

Seven

Spirit of Christ, Spirit of the World

ike Lewis Carroll's *Alice in Wonderland* and Jonathan Swift's *Gulliver's Travels*, L. Frank Baum's *The Wizard of Oz* is at once an enchanting children's fable and simultaneously a biting satire on the foibles of grown-up psychology and politics.** Briefly, in Baum's enchanted story four fellow travelers join interests to make their way through a magical land. In establishing their identity and solving their problems, they are transformed and much is revealed.

Baum may not have intended this, but I join those who see in the *Oz* story a parable for our country. First, Dorothy, the apple pie middle-American every-woman fresh from the prairie, feels more than a little lost. She is so far outside her comfort zone that she wants nothing more than to return home. She quickly teams up with the Scarecrow, her closest friend and natural ally, agrarian America seeking a brain to cope with a dizzying day when technology is revolutionizing familiar farm practices that had been virtually unchanged for centuries. Next comes the Tin Man, representing mechanized industrial America. He is confident and successful enough, but his progress is regularly impaired and even paralyzed because he lacks a heart. Finally, there is the belligerent but insecure Cowardly Lion, military America still awkward with its new imperial power, seeking courage enough to stop trying to roar and intimidate only to end up looking senseless and weak after the fact. (Toto the dog scampers about as simple, intuitive common sense, delightfully ahead of the other superior sentient creatures.) As we would say in today's parlance, each of these fellow travelers "has issues" they are working on.

How do they decide to deal with their issues? Almost reflexively, the answer rises within them: they go seek out a far-off amazing wizard who must surely have answers to their various problems. They quickly resolve to seek out this wonderful, wonderful wizard in the far off Emerald City. Both the slickness and the cluelessness of life in Oz bear an uncanny resemblance to life in Washington, D.C. And it is not until the end of the story, after incredibly heroic lengths by these four to prove themselves worthy of an audience with the great and powerful Oz, that we learn that the wizard's wizardry is as ordinary as a snake-oil salesman's smoke and mirrors.

At the story's close, Dorothy's companions are anticlimactically recognized for qualities and certified for achievements that Oz — like Washington — knows little about and had nothing to do with. And that somehow gets called empowerment, or at least gives them the status of having been "made official." But as the lighter-than-air balloon slips away and all seems lost for Dorothy, at that very nadir of her misfortune and the peak of her despair, she is surprised to learn it was within her power all along to do everything necessary to find her way home and assist her three friends.

This puzzling realization that famously frustrates children also satirizes a tendency within competent but insecure adults who look afar to exotic places and distant authorities for sanction and trajectory in finding their way. Tweaking this very human tendency — this pining after a reality check as we launch out into the world — is at the heart of the lesson that adults can find in Baum's story. It is also instructive for the church as we set out into the world to bring the witness of Christ to bear amid strange and challenging scenarios.

It was not necessary for Dorothy or (by implication) her three companions to sojourn long and far to be legitimized by a wizard who really wasn't such a wizard after all. They only imagined that they needed to, because they didn't know where else to begin. In order to find themselves, to hear their calling in life, and to be led forward toward purposeful and useful lives, they could have begun right where they were. Their first steps were already within their grasp the entire time they were begging for the help, sanction and direction of fancier powers posturing beyond the horizon. If only they had known that at the outset!

Begin Where You Are

One of the consistent impulses that I have regularly observed in five different churches and five different conferences over 27 years of local church ministry has been the question: what is happening in the national United Church of Christ headquarters? Or, similarly, what is happening in the national and world Christian ecumenical agencies? It is one of the first questions on the lips of UCC pastors as we gather informally over coffee in corridors at conferences or open our brown bag lunches at local UCC ministerial gatherings. People of other denominations undoubtedly ask each other the same question about their own denominations. And it is not a bad question. Connectedness in our rather fragmented polity is a good thing

What is bad, however, is when we suppose that, if the church of Jesus Christ is to find itself in its mission and outreach, it must necessarily look to some far off place where powerful but unknown experts preside. What is bad is when we assume that such as these have discerned grandiose schemes of spiritual strategies that are lost upon poor local church bumpkins with as pitifully few resources as ourselves.

What is bad is when we forget that the frontier and cutting edge of Christ's church is in truth the local church. The beauty and genius of our UCC polity, as it is in different ways in other mainline denominations, comes with the recognition of the dynamic intelligence and resourceful vitality of the local church in bringing the witness to Christ crucified and resurrected right where we live and work. These are the front lines in the work of God's reign. These are the trenches within which the war between good and evil is ultimately being waged, not on some far off horizon.

The wider church really exists more to empower and support the initiatives of the local church than for the local church to sit at the knee of the national church's higher consciousness. Indeed, in my view the wider church exists to take its lead from the local church more than the other way around. We are today relearning these rightful relationships after too many local church pilgrimages to Oz. The fact is that the largest of the UCC's predecessor churches, the Congregational church, did some of its best transformational outreach for centuries before the barest semblance of our national church representative gathering first came together in the 1830s.

All five of the practical theologians who have made the biggest difference in American church history — Jonathan Edwards, Horace Bushnell, Walter Rauschenbusch, Reinhold Niebuhr and Dr. Martin Luther King, Jr. — spent significant time as local church pastors. All five come from Protestant traditions where the accent is placed not upon Oz-like hierarchies and bureaucracies, more indicative of our Christendom past than our post-Christendom future. All five came from traditions (Congregational, Baptist, and German Evangelical) where the genius of the church — genius not just in thinking, but for action — locates itself in the local neighborhood church.

Let's face it, the local church has been the most basic unit of Christianity — from the house churches of the book of Acts to massive multiple-staff churches of today — for two millennia. We do well to lift that up before we start looking far beyond ourselves at glittering horizons for wiser or more powerful church agencies who will show us the way by instructing us in where human salvation lies.

This is not to say we should not be in touch with the associations, conferences, or synods of our wider denominations. We should. But it should be in the spirit that we can learn much from one another instead of making a more one-sided approach. It is to also say that the local church should be more reasonable and realistic in what we expect our wider denominations to accomplish on our behalf by way of mission and outreach. We cannot expect them to give us the moon and the stars, to remove the struggle of these difficult efforts and to burn away the mystery in which our church vocations get shrouded.

It is as though we need someone to tell us, like baby doctor Benjamin Spock counseling the skittish mothers of the mid-twentieth century, "You know more than you think." Begin right where you are. Recall the instincts imparted through the legacy of mothers and fathers, sisters and brothers in faith. Trust the still, small voice of holy hopefulness or righteous outrage or tender yearning for humankind rising up from within you where you now live. Do not pine after some big and booming voice of Oz that is in actuality only some concocter of potions behind a curtain.

Temptation of Oz Revisited

Beyond the mistake of wanting to look to large and distant denominational entities as a be-all and end-all, another way in which we sell short the gifts and possibilities of the local church is by looking too soon and too often to secular agencies to cure the ails of the world. Oz's satire would equally criticize the impulse within mainline churches like ours to go first to secular congresses and legislatures to address the painful and haunting issues of human need. We instinctively want to do this because we perceive these governmental bodies as so powerful and well-funded that they must possess some kind of "magic bullet" to resolve so many things. But here we make the same mistake as Dorothy and her three friends.

I mentioned in Chapter Two the story of my church staff in Columbus practically laughing at me for taking seriously Habitat for Humanity as a vehicle for addressing world poverty. This is not only an example of paradigm realignment, but also an illustration of the need to begin where we are rather than seeking grandiose solutions from larger far-off official bodies. Back in the mid-1980s, of course, Habitat's impact was more embryonic and potential than pervasive and obvious.

As my staff chided me for my trip and urged me to lobby Ohio or Washington instead, I remember getting angry, having to work to try to keep my cool. And this is what made me so angry: Could you imagine the twelve apostles responding to Jesus' commission to bring God's reign to the ends of the earth, choosing to start by trying to persuade the Roman Empire's Senate that they needed to spearhead this Spirit-led movement to proclaim Christ crucified and resurrected? Could you imagine those apostles starting within that belly of the imperial beast because a large, well-funded global entity had to be involved if the work had a chance to get done? Could you imagine the apostles trying to persuade senators that, for the reign of God to be established on earth, it would have to begin with and go through them? That it was up to the senators, through touching the lives of the poor and oppressed, to get the ball rolling to demonstrate that Jesus is Lord — these powerful men who had sworn loyalty to the affirmation that Caesar, not Jesus, is Lord?

And if we couldn't see that happening back with the apostles back in the days of the Roman empire, then why do we expect something similar to happen today under the aegis of the American empire? Aren't all empires pretty much the same in the final analysis, sad to say — killing for what they believe in instead of suffering and dying for what they believe in, as Jesus did? Wasn't it an empire that enslaved the people of Israel, an empire that gave the order for the crucifixion of Jesus? Why do we expect empires — even our own American empire — which have given God's people so much trouble over the centuries, suddenly to become champions of the work and creators of the new order proclaiming that Jesus is Lord? Some still labor under the illusion that America is basically a Christian nation. If nursing the illusion was more understandable decades ago, it makes less and less sense amid our imperial military agitations in the second millennium.

Other than wanting quick results and not having anything like faith in what is unseen demanded of us, why should we expect secular deliberative bodies to do our work for us? My staff colleagues looked at me like I was — at least theologically — from another planet. In a sense they were right. I was trying to get off the cold and dying planet of Christendom. To me, starting the outreach of the church by lobbying Congress makes about as much sense as Dorothy and her three friends expecting Oz to solve all of their problems and put their whole world aright.

In 1993 I left that Columbus church after almost eight years to serve a church in Colorado, and by then there were as many Habitat affiliates in the state of Ohio alone as there had been Habitat affiliates nationally when I arrived. That is how exponentially Habitat had grown in eight years. As for affordable housing for the poor created by the federal Department of Housing and Urban Development? I recall seeing the one — one! — house that HUD built as affordable housing in the entire state of Colorado in 1996. By now, Habitat for Humanity has built over 250,000 homes for God's people in need — working with governments obliquely, as it can, but striving to never get co-opted by governments' self-understanding and systems. So much for having to stop by great and powerful Oz before pursuing the dream of decent shelter for all of God's people.

Guerrillas of God's Grace

These final chapters of practical missiology seek to underscore how gifted the local church already is to take action right where God has situated us. With the faithfulness and wisdom and resources already at our disposal we are in a position to respond to realities like racism, illiteracy, hunger, exploitation, poverty, materialism, loneliness, hatefulness, consumerism, environmental degradation, ignorance, sexism, child abuse, and the rest of contemporary evils that haunt people and lead us to despair. Through word and deed we are equipped to confront the hopelessness that will always be pervasive wherever God's people seek to find their way through life apart from God.

And we need only exercise the spiritual discernments the church has exercised for centuries around these spiritual journeys outward. We need not wait for the go-ahead from some officially sanctioned far-off impressive body of specialists; we can abandon our human tendency to set our more tiny wristwatches by bigger clumsier clocks set upon grand stone towers even though our watches are more accurate. Why do we feel the need to look so far beyond ourselves to bigger people and places to do the work that we are ready to do and that God would have us do right here and now?

Our motto should be like that of those seminarians at the Haystack Meeting in western Massachusetts back in 1810. They owned nothing and had less experience in parish ministry than we do. Led by the Spirit, after the inspiration of a storm-interrupted prayer meeting, they launched their worldwide foreign mission initiative, proclaiming, "We Can If We Will." Today for us to say "we can if we will" again is not to elevate the positive thinking of the Little Engine That Could as sacred theology. It is to recognize that God is calling us to act right now where God has placed us and given us everything we need to do to make a beginning.

Notice that I say "to make a beginning." So often we don't start because we sense that within the foreseeable future we cannot do everything that needs to be done. But we don't need to. Taking our mark for action, we always do well to remind ourselves that it is God's job to save the world. We are not responsible for that. We are no good at rescuing humankind, but God's rescue mission launched in Jesus Christ is only beginning to unfold, is sufficient in all causes, and will be vindicated on the final day. I remember a church youth mission trip to Maine one year whose slogan was "all things are possible." That overestimating miss was a mile off, for the Christian message is that, "*with God*, all things are possible." And we had better keep that straight from beginning to end. What a difference a word makes!

Rather than saving the world — the weariness of the thought often paralyzes us before we begin — it is our job to do our own small part where God has placed us among neighbors in being part of the answer God has put forth in Jesus Christ. This is always an excellent alternative to our more familiar stance of waiting around for something to happen, waiting for someone bigger and more impressive to sanction and fund us, waiting until through the convergence of some unknown forces we are finally in the position to do "everything."

If this smells suspiciously like a continuation and elaboration of the "think big, start small" theme elucidated earlier, that is absolutely correct. So often we fail to make a beginning because we are waiting for some big and booming voice to tell us precisely what we are supposed to do (never mind that man behind the curtain!) and how we are supposed to go about it. Those expectations deafen us to the small voices locally crying out all around us, voices that go unanswered because they lack anything like officialdom. All that Jesus has asked of us is to look into the faces of God's children in need and see his own face.

That is all the sanction that we need to love our neighbor and to introduce the difference that God in Christ has made in ways both tangible and intangible. That, and the discernment of the gathered congregation to evaluate in which direction God would have us move right now, where God personally intends that we should go. These cues abound all around us for those who have eyes of faith to see and ears of faith to hear the leading of the Holy Spirit. How to transform policy-oriented boards and committees into spiritual discernment-grounded ministry teams is covered well in other books,[1] but it is at least worth mentioning here. If procedurally-obsessed boards and committees cannot in some sense also become mobile and responsive ministry teams, they will surprisingly and ironically often block the church's attempt to answer that still, small voice of God beckoning us. I have seen it in more than one church, but here is just one example.

Do Not Quench the Spirit

In the early 1980s, some refugees from Cambodia knocked on the door of Columbus' First Congregational Church UCC, which I later came to serve. Looking to our majestic neo-Gothic church (itself an Oz-like edifice) and seeing something like sanctuary, they approached the church's governing body and asked for help in adapting to a new environment. This was the epoch of the genocidal Pol Pot when millions perished and thousands of Cambodians became refugees, some fleeing to the United States. A pocket of them settled in downtown Columbus.

The official church council felt overwhelmed by their request for assistance, failed to see this hidden opportunity for ministry, and issued a flat no. "We would like to help you," was their carefully worded response to these broken, hopeful people, "but your needs are too great. We lack the resources. We would like to do something, but we would be in way over our heads. We are sorry, but goodbye and God bless you."

Still, these earnest and desperate Cambodians kept coming anyway, knocking on our doors, and asking for our help. Probably never having heard of it, they lived out the Parable of the Insistent Widow, who wouldn't let that reluctant judge alone. Their need was so great and their awareness of our potential to assist them was so compelling that they kept coming and entreating us. God bless them, their need was so acute and their motives so innocent they didn't know any better than to stop asking.

Within our board and committee church structures, it is sad how much housekeeping and how little spiritual discernment actually happens. But outside them? Grass roots members began to talk among themselves. They considered the needs of these refugees and realized that we could actually help them here and there. Assignments were made to those who possessed the skills that were precisely what the Cambodians sought. Piecemeal work became wholehearted and concerted. Before we knew it, almost despite ourselves and because of the Holy Spirit, our church became a bustling center for refugee resettlement. And the spontaneous generosity of that congregation, mobilized from the grass roots, was nothing less than remarkable.

Eventually, overcoming our initial rebuff, that church again gathered itself and eagerly addressed every dimension of these Cambodians' lives in a new world. They needed help finding apartments? The church found affordable apartments. They needed help with a new language? The church collaborated with the Roman Catholic diocese to form a program teaching English as a second language in our education wing — a program that went on to help thousands of Cubans, Haitians, and Romanians as well. Cambodian families needed help with driver's licenses or loans or math tutors or medical care or babysitting for their children? They needed help with the legal and tax implications of creating their own businesses? That church became truly the Church of Jesus Christ as it expertly saw to all of this and more.

The Cambodian families were so grateful, determined, industrious, and unified that their fortunes soared. True, we didn't do enough to welcome them within our worship life and offer them a spiritual center within their own distinctive ethnic praise of God. Nevertheless, miracles unfolded. More than one of their children became valedictorians of local graduating high school classes. Many of their businesses or trades quickly carved out niches and flourished. I recall taking my family to a wonderful restaurant founded by one of these Cambodian families. Though I had done practically nothing, I was treated royally, like long lost Prince Sihanouk, simply by virtue of being "the pastor" of the church which had cast its lot with them.

Jesus Is Coming, Look Busy

It is almost less important which front we move upon than that we get moving on one front or another, and interrupt the inertia that assumes nothing can be done, the despair that we cannot make a difference. Was your well-educated and well-heeled nephew jailed and treated horribly? God may be calling your church to a jail and prison ministry, or at least to address as a church how young people get harassed in ways that others do not. Are drugs a surprising new problem in your rural farm area? And you supposed that could only happen in the cities? Perhaps God intends your church to learn from city folk and create a center for recovering substance abusers out in farm America.

Are your youth bored with sitting around shopping malls all summer? Open to them possibilities beyond Disney World, even God's drama of redemption among struggling families in places like Maine, Louisiana, or South Dakota. Is immigrant labor, crucial to providing basic services that are taken for granted, being exploited and even demonized in your area? Perhaps they need a place where they can remember they are God's beloved children, praising God in the sanctuary you loan them for free as they organize their own church. And this is to say nothing of the bereaved, divorced, abused, or otherwise broken families where the heartfelt response of the people of God is no less a ministry of outreach.

Churches do not lack good will. We do not lack people power. We do not lack resources, be they ever so humble. We do not lack the awareness that in order truly to be the church, actions like these are our basic constitutive practices in following Christ. Deep down we know that we should be doing these things. And when we do them, people smile and remark with a sense of discovery, "Wow, that really feels like the church!" They are glimpsing the full human stature of the best possible reflection upon God that we could possibly be. When the church engages its mission and expresses itself in outreach, we tend to be at our very highest and best. And that is the place from which we want to do more living as the people of God.

So what do we lack? We lack imagination and leadership that sees these glorious possibilities before they can become a fuller response. And that requires faith — the faith that is the simple and venturesome and incorrigible trust that Christ is alive and out in the world waiting for us to join him in his transforming deeds of compassion, truth, and righteousness. We don't have to supply the power; it was established eternally in Jesus' death and resurrection. It is called the Holy Spirit. In this sense, such a faith — seeing godly responses into being among the neglected and forgotten — is what the church brings to the table of transforming society. It is this and not the driving of the public policy of a country, state, county, or town.

Inspiration is not only where we find it. It is where God beckons and sends us. And there are no coincidences in the life of the Holy Spirit, only providences. Inspiration is holy imagination unleashed on specific circumstances and details that we come across all the time. We must learn to see the world anew through the eyes of Jesus. Did you vacation on an isle off Central America only to learn from a chambermaid how sorely people are in need of a water project, dental care, or decent homes? Learn some Spanish, talk to others who know something about this area — most notably through wider church connections — and make a beginning by gaining a foothold in reaching out. Of course, people do this all of the time, dentists and doctors, carpenters and electricians, masons and plumbers, teachers and nurses. And they make all of the difference in the world in bringing alive the cause of Christ for those who can't see it.

Outreach as Though We Can Do No Other

As pastors and church leaders, we should develop relationships across our years of ministry with mission houses, para-church organizations, benevolent movements, and isolated pockets of godly goodness that we have taken to heart and believe to be something very special. Then when we move on to new churches, we should mention these relationships in ways that say to our hearers, "Love me, love my passion for God at work in the world. Here is where that passion gets acted out. Are you in?" Mark this territory even before you begin at your new church. We want to radiate this contagion from the very beginning, when we have leverage.

As part of this process, we should make clear in no uncertain terms that we bring these ongoing relationships and this agenda. Pastors talking with Search Committees should ask: Is the congregation ready to respond on fronts like these? Do you know that a significant portion of my time and your money will go in directions like these? Similarly, we should be ready to shuffle our own personal deck of mission partnerships and relationships as we discover that our new congregation has deep and dear relationships with mission partners. Putting this out front when we are new to a church stakes a claim and establishes an expectation that both leaders and congregation must subsequently live up to. And that is always healthy.

People ask all the time about the format and structure for raising funds for mission and outreach. Specifically, people ask about raising funds as a line on the budget (often as directed-giving for denominational or per capita support) versus raising funds through episodic and one-time appeals that get routed through mission partners, often non-denominational. Because the budget-based approach is more familiar and traditional, many within our churches assume it is more legitimate, more important, or somehow matters more in the eyes of God. They assume it is the only real way truly to honestly gauge the mission giving of a congregation. This was once true, but is no longer the case.

Patterns are changing in the post-Christendom church. In a day of escalating salary costs and benefits for maintaining a church staff, the mission budget is often the first place raided by the Finance Committee to balance the budget. Sad to say, that simple reality likely will not change anytime soon. And so if your church is able to protect and maintain its budget line items dedicated toward outreach, that is outstanding. Congratulations, well done, good and faithful servants. But realize that you are in the minority of churches. And know that these times, they're a changin'.

We must remain resourceful in inviting support for outreach when the old familiar ways no longer work. After all, when all is said and done, Jesus doesn't give a hoot whether the money we have raised to dig a well in the mountains of Panama was raised through a traditional budgetary process or through a passionate appeal of a church member who was moved by the sight or thought of women exerting tremendous effort to carry potable water in cans on their heads for many kilometers.

In the funding of outreach, change means that many people in our churches want an approach toward giving that is less institutional and more of a grass roots movement. The cynical will complain that we are de-emphasizing outreach by not "locking it in" the budgetary process, as we do Sunday School curricula, fuel, office expenses, and the like. But it is also true that we live in a day when people want a more direct and personal relationship with these forms of outreach than routing money through layers of agencies typically allows. And people will often be willing to give more generously — giving, say, the specific amount for the pump in that mountain well — if the action can be interpreted in ways that are more direct and personal. Most importantly, this episodic approach bears more promise to involve the people of the church directly in the work of the outreach, which is a supreme goal, bearing great hope for transformation on all sides.

So if the question is whether we raise the funds through existing budgetary processes and route them through the hierarchies of denominations and global councils of churches, or whether we make regular personal appeals toward outreach, replete with publicity, envelopes in the pews, stories of people who know first hand of the need, and who have worked side by side with potential beneficiaries? The answer, of course, is yes, we do both.

We are in a historical time of transition in this regard. But at this moment, history is probably tilting toward the side of the latter. So don't be surprised if the institutional Christendom budget-based approach must yield more and more to a free-form, personal, grass-roots movement approach with the opportunity to involve people directly. In some ways the latter is much harder work than underwriting a budget line item, but in other ways it is also much more vital and personal.

People also ask about more regional and local forms of outreach versus farther-flung global mission efforts. Often this talk cloaks the unstated desire that everything we give should remain within the United States of America. People will quote the "Bible" they carry in their heads, "Charity begins at home." Of course, this sentence does not appear in any Christian Bible. And the truth is that Jesus said something close to the opposite: The more self-disinterested our spirit of giving and service, the better and the holier it is. We should be careful that these voices are not voices of demagoguery, and that these voices not gain credence in our congregations. Biblical preaching and teaching — breaking down worldly limits and separations — are the effective antitoxin here.

This much is clear: By drawing us out in commanding us to love our neighbor — the basic Christian imperative for following our living Lord out into a world in need — Jesus was not thinking along the types of lines that nation-states draw as borders. Just the opposite. Jesus went out of his way to explode such boundaries by telling a parable of a priest, a Levite, and a despised Samaritan. The latter foreigner was out of his element, in an alien place, but managed to do the will of God where the more local and more socially approved priest and Levite failed. Jesus would have us respond to human need wherever it is acute, wherever ache the bodies, minds, souls, and spirits of God's children in need. For there can be no joy for any of us until there is joy enough for such as these.

At the same time we live in a world very different from Jesus' day — a globe dramatically shrunk. So the command to love our neighbor has expanded commensurately to encompass peoples and languages and cultures that might not necessarily bear the Good Housekeeping stamp of approval that would endorse them as white suburban people just like us. (Yes, despite all of our talk of diversity, the truth is that many mainline churches overwhelmingly remain white and suburban.) If an abjectly poor family in the Yucatán is physically closer to where I live than a more moderately poor family in Seattle (as happens to be the case by my own geography), should I favor and serve the family in Seattle because of how nation-states have drawn their lines? Not always, according to Jesus' calculations. And this doesn't even touch upon how dramatically much more impact for good a thousand dollars can make in the Yucatán than it can in Seattle.

People ask what kind of partnerships with religious agencies and benevolent organizations our local churches should strike, especially when it comes to the giving of the funds we raise. Where should we begin? I see youth groups doing car washes all the time for the cancer society and the kidney foundation, for the fund to build a new high school athletic facility and to send the concert band to Europe. We should be careful here. Remember, witness is the watchword. Even more important than any tangible good we do is how what we do proclaims the living presence of Jesus Christ in the world, the transforming power of the crucified and resurrected One. That the bodies through whom we work embrace Christ crucified and resurrected is essential to the transmission of this message.

That doesn't mean that everything that we do has to be strictly Christian or through the auspices of the church. Amnesty International does some amazing things, for example, and it will welcome the grass roots letter-writing of our people. Also, the many worthy faith-based community building organizations in the hardscrabble parts of urban areas frequently embrace many faiths, not just Christianity. But the first impulse and the lion's share of our giving and support should go through distinctively Christian and ecumenical channels. Otherwise, we not only end up feeling like the Rotary Club or the Kiwanis, we end up acting like them. Still, sorting this out and balancing these interests will never be easy for church mission bodies.

Habitat for Humanity (to mention this paradigm changer one more time!) is an example of striking this balance well, avoiding becoming the Elks Club while also avoiding becoming exclusivist and imperialistic in their faith. Yes, they are an avowedly Christian organization, but they welcome workers of all faiths and of no faith. They don't sell their no-interest houses only to Christians — that would violate the Spirit of Christ. But with every house they build they do insist upon a dedication service where a Bible is presented to the new homeowners. And that is not optional. They ingeniously retain their Christian identity while embracing and welcoming into the effort as many backgrounds as possible as they recruit workers and find recipient families.

One Last Thought

As the local church, we know more than we think. We are *ecclesia* — in Greek, literally, those called out of the world into the church. But no sooner are we called out of the world and into the church than we are sent by the soon-to-be-ascended Christ out of the church and back into the world. Jesus foresaw a church constantly on the move and gave us an Advocate to keep us moving.

116

We bear a message that is as big as the redemption of humankind, the reconciliation of heaven and earth. Discerning the places, the strategies, the words, and these deeds by which we make this proclamation is not as easy as clicking the heels of ruby slippers. But everything we need to stake our claim in the reign of God by reaching out to our neighbors has been given to us in abundance right where we live right now. That simple abundance — material and spiritual — too often remains buried and hidden. Can we uncover these riches for the benefit of all parties and share them with the passion and zest they deserve?

We have more opportunity to witness to the living Lord and participate in the resurrection of Christ than we recognize in our day-to-day lives. The stage is set for the drama of humankind's unfolding redemption in Christ to play out right where we live. A role has been assigned to us. Discerning our role is like figuring out the part specially assigned to us in this play, described on a sheet in an envelope, without being able to open that envelope. How can we get inside of that envelope, get inside of the mind of Christ, without tearing it open? It requires the resources of the entire community where Christ has taken up residence. We cannot do this alone.

God has set us on fire that the world might watch us burn with goodness, compassion, truthfulness, righteousness, justice, generosity of spirit, and peace. God has set us on fire that, in burning with the Spirit of God yet not being consumed, the world might find its way toward the light and warmth of dwelling in communion with God. Nothing could be better than that. This is no grim obligation of grinding duty. This is the ultimate joy that Jesus Christ came to bring, and brought abundantly. That abundance for all would mean scarcity for none. That every last person is caught up in this embrace and no one is left behind. That nothing should separate us from the love of God in Christ Jesus.

Notes

Chapter One

1. Homiletics Online, http://www.homileticsonline.com/subscriber/illustration_search.asp?keywords=parable&imageField2.x=8&imageField2.y=4 (accessed April 24, 2007).

2. Exodus 3: 1–12.

3. "Trinity UCC in Chicago: Faith and Growth Together," *United Church News*, January/February 1997, 1, 7.

4. Stanley Hauerwas, *Unleashing the Scripture: Freeing the Bible from Captivity to America* (Abingdon Press: Nashville, Tenn., 1993), 1.

5. James 2: 26.

6. Elizabeth O'Connor, *Journey Inward, Journey Outward* (Harper and Row: New York, 1968).

7. Matthew 25: 31–46.

8. Anthony Campolo, *Wake Up America!: Answering God's Radical Call While Living in the Real World* (Zondervan: Grand Rapids, Mich., 1991), 147.

9. The Great Commission is this:

> And Jesus came and said to them, "All authority in heaven and on earth has been given to me. Go therefore and make disciples of all nations, baptizing them in the name of the Father and of the Son and of the Holy Spirit, and teaching them to obey everything that I have commanded you. And remember, I am with you always, to the end of the age." (Matt. 28: 18–20).

And this is the Great Compassion:

> "Then the king will say to those at his right hand, 'Come, you that are blessed by my Father, inherit the kingdom prepared for you from the foundation of the world; for I was hungry and you gave me food, I was thirsty and you gave me something to drink, I was a stranger and you welcomed me, I was naked and you gave me clothing, I was sick and you took care of me, I was in prison and you visited me.'" (Matt. 25: 34–36).

Chapter Two

1. Wikipedia Foundation, Inc., http://en.wikipedia.org/wiki/Parzival (accessed April 6, 2007).

2. H. Richard Niebuhr, *Christ and Culture* (Harper: New York, 1951).

3. John Howard Yoder, *The Politics of Jesus: Vicit Agnus Noster* (Eerdmans: Grand Rapids, Mich., 1972).

4. Stanley Hauerwas and William H. Willimon, *Resident Aliens: Life in the Christian Colony* (Abingdon Press: Nashville, Tenn., 1989), 44–46.

Chapter Three

1. Martin Luther King, Jr., *The Autobiography of Martin Luther King, Jr.*, ed. Clayborne Carson (Warner Books: New York, 1998), 74.

2. Ibid., 75.

3. Ibid.

4 . Charles Marsh, *The Beloved Community: How Faith Shapes Social Justice, From the Civil Rights Movements To Today* (Basic Books: New York, 2005), 35.

5. Isaiah 29: 13.

6. Anthony B. Robinson, "The Procedural Church," private manuscript in files of author, July 14, 1997, 2.

7. Ibid., 4.

8. Mark 6: 7–12.

9. See Lillian Daniel's book, *Tell It Like It Is: Reclaiming the Practice of Testimony* (Alban Institute: Herndon, Va., 2006).

10. Loren B. Mead, *The Once and Future Church: Reinventing the Congregation for a New Mission Frontier* (Alban Institute: Washington, D.C., 1991).

11. "Salvadorian vision clinic serves thousands, founded by UCC ophthalmologist," *United Church News*, August/September 2006, A17.

12. Clarence Jordan, *The Cotton Patch Version of Matthew and John* (Association Press: New York, 1970).

13. Henri J.M. Nouwen, *Reaching Out: The Three Movements of the Spiritual Life* (Doubleday: Garden City, N.Y., 1975), 43.. Italics are mine.

Chapter Four

1. Luke 16: 10a.

2. Quoted in L. Gregory Jones, "Faith Matters," *The Christian Century*, August 23, 2005, 29.

3. Ibid.

4. Emily Dickinson, "Tell all the Truth but tell it slant." Word Front, LLC, http://poetry.poetryx.com/poems/3070 (accessed April 24, 2007).

5. Gus and Sue Kuether, personal communication with author, February 1984.

6. O'Connor, *Journey Inward, Journey Outward*, 113.

7. Two good examples are Miroslav Volf and Dorothy C. Bass, eds., *Practicing Theology: Beliefs and Practices in Christian Life* (W. B. Eerdmans: Grand Rapids, Mich., 2002), and Craig Dykstra, *Growing in the Life of Faith: Education and Christian Practices* (Geneva Press: Louisville, Ky., 1999).

8. O'Connor, *Journey Inward, Journey Outward*, 18–19.

9. Ibid., 20.

10. The Gallup Organization, http://www.gallup.com/ (accessed April 24, 2007).

Chapter Five

1. "Centurymarks," *The Christian Century*, August 22, 2006, 6.

2. Acts 1: 8.

3. Mark 4: 30-32.

4. As told in Marsh, *Beloved Community* , 194.

5. Gene Rivers, quoted in John Leland, "Savior of the Streets," *Newsweek*, June 1, 1998, 25.

6. Gene Rivers, quoted in Marsh, *Beloved Community*, 196.

7. Gene Rivers, quoted in Omar M. McRoberts, *Streets of Glory: Church and Community in a Black Urban Neighborhood* (University of Chicago: Chicago 2003), 119.

8. Gene Rivers, quoted in Marsh, *Beloved Community*, 196.

9. Marsh, *Beloved Community*, 196.

10. Rydell Payne, lecture to the Project on Lived Theology at the

University of Virginia, April 22, 2003, cited in Marsh, *Beloved Community*, 196.

11. A transcript of Amy L. Sherman's October 13, 2001 presentation to the Theology of Community Building Workgroup at the University of Virginia can be found at The Project on Lived Theology, http://www.livedtheology.org/pdfs/Sherman.pdf, 2 (accessed April 6, 2007).

12. Ibid., 3, 9-10.

13. Ibid., 3.

14. Luke 16: 20 ff.

15. Ezekiel 47: 1–12.

Chapter Six

1. Luke 18: 18–25.

Chapter Seven

1. See, for example, George Garna, *The Habits of Highly Effective Churches: Being Strategic in your God-Given Ministry* (Regal Books: Ventura, Calif., 1999), and E. Stanley Ott, *Transform Your Church with Ministry Teams* (William B. Eerdmans Pub.: Grand Rapids, Mich., 2004).

Other books from The Pilgrim Press

Leadership for Vital Congregations
Anthony B. Robinson
ISBN 978-0-8298-1712-6/paper/128 pages/$12.00
   This is an essential leadership tool for clergy and lay leaders who wish to revitalize their leadership style and approach to become more effective leaders. It offers: functional strategies to lead; information on developing as a spiritual leader; ways that the congregation can understand the importance of leadership; and much more.

Worship for Vital Congregations
Talitha Arnold
ISBN 978-0-8298-1729-4/paper/96 pages/$12.00
   Arnold shares her current congregation's remarkable success story during her leadership, such as: membership has more than doubled; programs in children's and youth ministry and adult education are flourishing; worship services are offered both in Spanish and English; and sign language for the hearing impaired is offered. She offers functional strategies to lead worship, information on how to develop as a spiritual leader and ways in which the congregation can understand the importance of worship and much more.

Can this Church Live?
A Congregation, Its Neighborhood, and Social Transformation
Donald Matthews
ISBN 0-8298-1648-8/paper/112 pages/$14.00
This resource chronicles the story of a church that had an opportunity to thrive in the midst of a community that greatly changed it demographics. Matthews ditects readers through the painful process he experienced with the pastor and church leaders as they faced a harsh dilemma – can or will a predominately white church embrace and welcome the people of color who live within the community?

The Generation Driven Church
Evangelizing Boomers, Busters and Millennials
William and Le Etta Benke
ISBN 0-8298-1509-0/paper/128 pages/$13.00

The Benkes seek to revitalize the ministries of small and mid-size churches by helping them to adjust to the changing culture. It also offers strategic approaches that will re-orient ministries to attract younger generations and take churches with an "inward focus," (churches devoid of conversion growth because of the absence of meaningful outreach to un-churched adults who comprise the post-modernist cultures) to an "outreach focus."

Behold I Do a New Thing
Transforming Communities of Faith
C. Kirk Hadaway
ISBN 0-8298-1430-2/paper/160 pages/$15.00

Recent talk and thinking about congregations concentrate on declining church attendance. Author Kirk Hadaway thinks an important part of the conversation is missing – how can churches, in spite of the decline, remain engaged in the mission of transforming lives? Looking at churches in new ways and holding new expectations will allow churches leadership to guide congregations in the journey where transformation and renewal is constant and embraced.

How to Get Along with Your Pastor
Creating Partnership for Doing Ministry
George B. Thompson, Jr.
ISBN 978-0-8298-17113-3/paper/144 pages/$17.00

Statistics show that approximately 1,300 American pastors unwillingly leave their congregations each month. These sudden changes have negative long-term effects on both the pastor and congregation. Thompson believes it is extremely important to find practical, easy-to-understand ways to train pastors and churches on how to approach disagreement constructively.

How to Get Along with Your Church
Creating Cultural Capital for Ministry
George B. Thompson Jr.
ISBN 0-8298-1437-X/paper/176 pages/$17.00

This resource incorporates Thompson's research and observations on pastoring a church. He finds that the pastors who are most successful in engaging their parishioners are the ones who develop "cultural capital" within their congregations, meaning that they invest themselves deeply into how their church does its work and ministries.

Gifts of Many Cultures
Worship Resources for the Global Community
Maren C. Tirabassi and Kathy Wonson Eddy
ISBN 0-8298-1029-3/paper/336 pages/$20.00

This book is a moving collection of liturgical resources from the global community that is designed to enrich the worship life of congregations in all denominations. It is an anthology of original prayers, stories and readings for sermons, invocations, calls to worship, confessions, and others resources that can be used around the seasons of the church year.

Legal Guide for Day-to-Day Church Matters
A Hand Book for Pastors and Church Leaders
Cynthia S. Mazur and Ronald K. Bullis
ISBN 0-8298—0990-2/paper/148 pages/$10.00

This book belongs on every pastor's desk because the church is not exempt from the growing number of lawsuits filed each year. The authors are clergy as well as attorneys.

To order these or any other books from The Pilgrim Press call or write to:

The Pilgrim Press
700 Prospect Avenue East
Cleveland, Ohio 44115-1100

Phone orders: 1-800-537-3394 • Fax orders: 216-736-2206
Please include shipping charges of $6.00 for the first book and $0.75 for each additional book.
Or order from our web sites at www.pilgrimpress.com and www.ucpress.com.

Prices subject to change without notice.